Contents

KU-243-354

UNIVERSITY
CARDIFF
31124445
372.6044/KS2/Bar
INFORMATION SERVICE

Introduction

Developing Literacy supports the teaching of reading and writing by providing a series of activities to develop essential skills in reading and spelling: word recognition and phonics. The activities are designed to be carried out in the time allocated to independent work during the Literacy Hour and therefore should be relatively 'teacher-free'. The focus is on children investigating words and spelling patterns, generating their own words in accordance with what they have learned and, if possible, recognising and devising rules and strategies to enable them to become independent in their recording and further investigation of language.

The activities presented in **Developing Literacy** support the learning objectives of the National Literacy Strategy at word-level. Each book:
- includes activities which focus on phonics, spelling, word recognition and vocabulary;
- develops children's understanding of sound-spelling relationships;
- helps children to extend their vocabulary by challenging them to talk about and investigate the meanings of words which they find difficult;
- promotes independent work during the Literacy Hour;
- provides extension activities on each page which reinforce and develop what the children have learned;
- includes brief notes for teachers on most pages.

Some of the activities focus on the high/medium frequency words listed in the National Literacy Strategy's *Framework for Teaching*. These are lists of words which need to be recognised on sight. At Key Stage 1, they are words which the children need to know in order to tackle even very simple texts. Some are regular but others, such as 'said' and 'water', do not follow regular phonic spelling patterns. At Key Stage 2, there is an additional list of medium frequency words which children often have difficulty in spelling.

The activities are presented in a way which requires children to read the words rather than just guessing the answers or 'filling in the spaces'. Sometimes they are asked to turn over the sheet and then write a list of words, or a partner could read the words aloud for them to write. Working with partners or in groups is encouraged so that children can check one another's reading and co-operate to complete the activities or play games. It is also useful for the children to show their work to the rest of the class and to explain their answers during the plenary session in order to reinforce and develop their own learning and that of others in the class.

Children need to 'Look, Say, Cover, Write and Check' (LSCWCh) words on a regular basis in order to learn their spellings. This has been indicated by the following logo:

It is essential that children learn the habit of looking up and checking words in a dictionary. This has been indicated by the following logo:

Use a dictionary.

Extension

Each activity sheet ends with a challenge (**Now try this!**) which reinforces and extends the children's learning and provides the teacher with an opportunity for assessment. Where children are asked to carry out an activity, the instructions are clear to enable them to work independently, for example,
- Find **four** other words for each of the letter strings.

The teacher may decide to amend this before photocopying, depending on his or her knowledge of the children's abilities and speed of working.

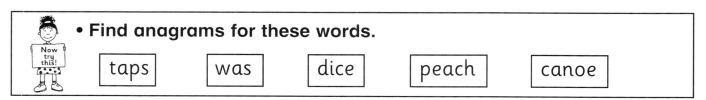

- **Find anagrams for these words.**

| taps | was | dice | peach | canoe |

Organisation

For many of the activities it will be useful to have an easily accessible range of dictionaries, thesauruses, fiction and non-fiction books, coloured pencils, counters, scissors and squared paper available. Several activities can be re-used to provide more practice in different letters or sounds, by masking the words and/or letters and replacing them with others of your choice.

To help teachers to select appropriate learning experiences for their pupils, the activities are grouped into sections within each book. The pages are **not** intended to be used in the order in which they appear in the books.

The teacher should select the appropriate pages to support the work in progress. Some children may be weak in areas which were covered in previous years. If so, teachers can refer to the **Developing Literacy** book for the previous year to find appropriate activity sheets, which may be adapted, to practise those areas. For more able children, the teacher may want to adapt the activity sheets by masking the words and letters and replacing them with more demanding examples.

Many activities will be completed entirely on the activity sheets. On others, particularly in the extension activities, the children will need to work either on the back of the page, on a separate sheet of paper or in an exercise book.

It is useful for children to keep their own word banks containing the new words they have learned. These could be general or for a specific topic on which the class is working. Children should be encouraged to make a note of any words they find difficult so that they can add them to the word bank. The class could also have a word wall display to which they can add new words.

Structure of the Literacy Hour

The recommended structure of the Literacy Hour for Key Stage 2 is as follows:

Whole class introduction	15 min	Shared text work (balance of reading and writing) in which the teacher reads or writes a piece of text with the class, to elicit participation in discussion of the topic to be taught.
Whole class activity	15 min	Focused word work in which the children contribute to a teacher-led activity arising from the whole class introduction.
Group work Independent work (rest of class)	20 min	The teacher works with groups of children on guided text work. The other children could work independently, for example, from the **Developing Literacy** activity sheets or on other reading or writing work.
Whole class plenary session	10 min	The teacher leads a review of what has been learned by consolidating teaching points, reviewing, reflecting and sharing the children's ideas and the results of their work.

The following flow chart shows an example of the way in which an activity from this book can be used to achieve the required organisation of the Literacy Hour.

ou, ow, or, aw (pages 29-32)

Whole class introduction   15 min

After reading a shared text, for example, a poem such as *The North Wind doth blow and we shall have snow*, and investigating the meaning of any unfamiliar words, the teacher asks the children to come forward and circle **ow** words which rhyme, such as 'snow' and 'blow'. The children brainstorm and the teacher scribes as many words as possible which make the same sound using the same letters. The children use and discuss the term 'phoneme'. Note any exceptions, where **ow** makes a sound which does not rhyme with 'snow'.

Whole class activity   15 min

Look carefully at any exceptions, such as growl. Rhyme by analogy, for example, how, howl. Make lists for the class word wall to be used later. Which other letters make the same sound as **ow** in snow, and **ow** in growl? List examples. Allow the children to circle the phonemes in the words and reach the conclusion that the same phoneme may be represented by different letters.

Independent work   20 min

Give groups differentiated activities. One group could play with **ou/ow** cards to match words to pictures, make words, list them, collect words containing only one of the phonemes, and so on. Other groups could extend to **or/aw** cards using the same principle or use all the cards to distinguish between all the sounds and list words in appropriate categories. Stress that the children should be using the Look, Say, Cover, Write and Check procedure to learn the words. Children in higher ability groups should be looking for common characteristics to formulate rules, for example, does **ou** ever come at the beginning of a word?

Group work   20 min

The teacher works with at least one group on guided text work.

Whole class plenary session   10 min

Children from each group tell the rest of the class what they have noticed and learned and write new words on the word wall. The teacher monitors the learning and assesses children's achievements to ensure that the work for the next Literacy Hour is appropriate and meaningful.

Teachers' notes

Very brief notes are provided at the foot of most pages. They give ideas for maximising the effectiveness of the activity sheets. They may make suggestions for the whole-class introduction, the plenary session or, possibly, follow up work using an adapted version of the activity sheet. Before photocopying, these notes could be masked.

Teachers' note This is an example of a letter string which has many different sounds. The children should practise writing the letter strings to encourage the flowing cursive style and to reinforce the relationship of the letters **ough**.

Developing Literacy Year 4
© A & C Black 1998

Using the activity sheets

Brief information is given here about the work within each section of **Developing Literacy Year 4.** Suggestions are also given for additional activities.

Spelling strategies (pages 9-25)

Activities in this section ask the children to investigate spelling, play with words, generate new words according to rules, and record what they find difficult. In this way, the children should become more independent in their spelling and not have to ask the teacher each time they think they cannot spell a word. The children need to be able to work independently during the Literacy Hour, or the management issues for the teacher, working closely with a group at all times, will be too difficult for high quality interaction to take place.

A word tree (page 9) provides a format on which to make collections of words about certain subjects, as specified in the *Framework for Teaching.* It also gives teachers the opportunity to monitor difficult spellings in subject areas such as geography or history.

Building words (page 10) encourages children to notice that some words have a root and that the root can be built on to. It is often a good idea to give the children the concept of spelling being like playing with blocks which fit together. If they have the correct blocks and can use other strategies in this book, such as the use of syllables, they can construct words accurately and spell similar words by analogy. The children could investigate the spelling of words which end in **e** when they word-build. What happens if a word ends in **y**? Can they generate words, work out common characteristics and find a rule?

Spelling with your hands (pages 11) uses sign language to spell words. It can be developed by asking the children to invent or use their own codes for spelling and to test them on others in the class. It should be linked closely with dictionary work and work on alphabetical order. **Police spelling** (page 12) and **Telephone numbers** (page 13) are fun activities in which the children are asked to think carefully about the individual letters which make up words.

There is fun and magic in language and the children should enjoy experimenting with it. Pages 14-21 are enjoyable activities designed to encourage the children to investigate the structure of words and to develop independent spelling strategies. Entire small words within larger words can be investigated, to develop a positive attitude towards language as a creative tool. Who can find the largest number of words? A special class word wall could be created to allow the children to spend any spare moments adding words to the lists. Making new words from the letters of a word can also form the basis of a challenge and can encourage dictionary and thesaurus work. The children are encouraged to deconstruct words rather than thinking of each word as a unit. For children who cannot complete a whole page, the pages can be cut up and used in easier ways, for example, for matching pictures to words, or simply by giving the children only a part of a page.

The aim of the following pages is to give the children practice in using a variety of dictionaries. They can be book-based or IT-based. The most important thing is that the children develop independence in their investigation of the spelling of words. You should have a variety of dictionaries available, ranging from simple children's dictionaries to those intended for adults. The children should be investigating options other than that of always asking the teacher!

Dictionary pages 1 and 2 (pages 22-23) test the children's knowledge of alphabetical order to three and four letters. A similar format could be used with children who have difficulty in finding their way around a dictionary: use only one word beginning with each letter. Word derivation and the use of an etymological dictionary could be developed in **Number words** (page 24), through prefixes with Latin and Greek derivations.

The relationship between sound and spelling is introduced in **Funny alphabets quiz** (page 25), which leads the children on to the activities in the next section on phonological awareness.

Spelling conventions and rules (pages 26-52)

Activities in this section are designed to give the children confidence and to help them to develop strategies in building words from letters, parts of words and words from sounds.

Difficult words (from page 26) focuses on the particular sounds and letter patterns which children find difficult. This gives them the opportunity to investigate the patterns, to check them using a dictionary and to write the words correctly. It also uses the idea of mnemonics to help them to remember these words.

Ugh! ough words (page 27) and **Letter strings are** and **and** (page 28) contain activities concerning common letter strings. Success in this area can be linked to work on analogy, for example, if you can spell **night**, you can spell **right** and **fight**. However, this is not the case with some letter strings, such as **ough**. The idea is not to hide the fact that there is no rule, but to allow the children to investigate it and to be aware of the problem. Work on letter strings should be linked to handwriting as the strings themselves provide good practice in letter formation and in reinforcing the pattern of letters which always come together. The children must be given the opportunity to investigate words, categorise any patterns, generate new examples by analogy and then formulate a rule if they can see one. In this way, spelling becomes more fun and less of a chore.

In **ou, ow, or** and **aw** (pages 29-32) words and pictures are provided to be used as a flexible resource for games and individual work. The flow chart on page 5 shows how these could be used. In **er, ir, or, ur** (page 33) and **Second phoneme relay** (page 34) the children can see that one sound (phoneme) can be represented by different letters (graphemes).

Homophones (page 35) demonstrates that some words sound exactly the same but are spelled differently and mean something very different. If they are brought to the children's attention as a peculiarity of language the children are more likely to be able to deal with them and learn to spell the alternatives. The words in the extension activities bring to light the fact that there are sometimes three alternatives. The difficulty of learning rules about sounds is also brought out in **Space invaders** (page 36) and **Word birds** (page 37), where the same letters make several different sounds. The children need to investigate the letters surrounding the sound and see if they can work out under what circumstances each sound is made. If the words are on display, reference can be made to them as a text during shared and guided reading.

In **Plurals revision**, **Plurals maths** and **Strange plurals** (pages 38-40), **Verb endings 1, 2, 3** (pages 41-43) and **Tense changes** (page 44), word-level activities are linked with sentence-level activities. These can be somewhat simpler than overtly phonological activities, as in most cases rules can be made and learned, for example, concerning plurals. What spelling strategies can the children be taught to help them develop independence in their writing? There are always exceptions in the English language and these can be made the most of in a fun way as in **Strange plurals** (page 40).

Locomotion solution (page 45), **Word wheel** (page 46), **Conundrums** (page 47) and **Making words** (page 50) deal with the tricky issue of the inflectional endings **tion, ial, ious**, where the sound of the word bears no relationship to the usual letter sounds on the page. George Bernard Shaw fought against traditional English spelling and noted the need for an easier phonetic alternative. His example to prove the problem was that **fish** could be spelled **ghoti**: **f = gh** as in enou**gh**; **i = o** as in w**o**men; **sh = ti** as in atten**ti**on. Do not be afraid to give the children difficult words to deal with. They can use their dictionary skills and enjoy investigating them.

There is considerable work on syllabic patterns and syllable structures of words in **Syllable snakes** (page 48) and **Syllable beavers** (page 49), as it is an effective way for children to build up and spell difficult words. If they realise that certain sounds (for example, **tion**) are themselves syllables, and can spell those syllables, they can add them correctly to the other syllables (the building block principle). **Making words** (page 50) tests the children's ability to make three-syllable words from separate syllables. This work builds upon and reinforces the word work of previous years. **Cockney rhyming slang** (page 51) and **Rhymes** (page 52) focus on rhyming words and the different spelling of the same sounds.

Vocabulary extension (page 53-64)

Mnemonics (page 53) helps children to devise their own strategies for learning the spelling of tricky words, particularly the high frequency words from the *Framework for Teaching*. Interesting visual classroom displays can provide a pictorial reminder of mnemonics, for example, a **hat** can be drawn on top of w**hat**. **'Nice' words, 'Said' words, 'Big' words** and **'Hot' words** (pages 54-57) concentrate on overused words and the need to vary vocabulary according to descriptive context. More difficult activities focus on differentiating levels of meaning in synonyms and encouraging the children to put their words into an appropriate context, for example, what is the difference in meaning between cold, freezing and glacial? When would it be appropriate to use these words accurately in their writing? Much of this work will arise from shared text work at the beginning of the Literacy Hour, and will be developed in shared and guided writing, especially in poetry. Use computers where possible to change and edit work more easily. Many computers have their own word bank facility or a thesaurus. **Verb wordsearch, Time wordsearch** and **Position and direction wordsearch** (pages 58-60) encourage the children to become familiar with, and learn to spell, these words.

Compound word flowers (page 61) requires the children to think of words in 'chunks'. If they can spell one part of the word, it becomes easier for them to extend and develop their spelling knowledge.

Inventing new words machine (page 62) gives the children the chance to experiment with making words from sections. The words may not exist in a dictionary but the nature of language is ever changing and yesterday's slang is today's standard English, for example 'computer-friendly'. This also links into work with language derivation and new words from technology or from other cultures becoming more important. **Jigsaw words** (page 63) gives children the opportunity to carry out the same kind of activity but using real word roots. Large words can be made up from entire, smaller ones. **Endings dice** (page 64) is a game in which children can choose and investigate words to which an ending can be added. Discuss with the children the correct use of 'die' for the singular.

Answers

Pages for which answers have been provided have been marked in the Teachers' notes with an asterisk (*).

Spelling with your hands (page 11):
balloon, suddenly, children, morning, important

Police spelling (page 12):
Following a number of young men.
Accident between High Street and station

Telephone numbers (page 13):
Dentist, bank, airport, library, hospital

Words within words (page 14):
important: imp, port, tan, an, ant
teacher: tea, teach, each, ache, he, her
introduction: in, trod, rod, duct, on
Christopher: Chris, Christ, is, stop, to, top, he, her

Record breaker (page 16):
The six letter word is **height**.

Animal anagrams (page 17):
fish, chicken, seal, tiger, monkey, kitten,
elephant, giraffe, tadpole, puppy

Word robots (page 18):
wolf: fowl, flow
meat: mate, team, tame
live: vile, veil, evil

item: mite, time
leap: peal, pale
smile: slime, miles, limes
spot: stop, post, pots, opts
steal: stale, slate, teals, tales, least

Lemons and melons (page 19):
mile - lime
rats - star
vowels - wolves
calm - clam
pests - steps
shrub - brush
petal - plate
words - sword
palm - lamp
taps - spat
was - saw
dice - iced
peach - cheap
canoe - ocean

Word magic (page 20):
mat, rat, rag, rug
him, hem, her
warm, ward, card, cord, cold
ship, chip, chap, chat, coat, boat
cat, cot, cog, dog, dot, rot, rat

Conundrums (page 47):
delicious, conscious, spacious,
vicious, precious, gracious

Glossary of terms used

analogy Recognising a word, phoneme or pattern in known words and applying this to new, unfamiliar words.
ascender The part of a letter which projects upwards, for example, in **b**, **d**, **h** and **k**.
blending Running together individual phonemes in pronunciation.
cluster A combination of consonant sounds before or after a vowel (or 'y' used as a vowel),
for example, **spr**ay, **cr**y, ru**st**.
descender The part of a letter which projects downwards, for example, in **g**, **j**, **p** and **y**.
grapheme The written representation of a sound which may consist of one or more letters.
homonyms Words which are spelled the same, have the same pronunciation, but a different meaning, for example,
Wave good-bye to your cousin. Watch out for the tidal **wave**!
homographs Words which are spelled the same, pronounced differently and mean something different, for example, **bow**, **wind**.
homophones Words which sound the same but mean something different and are spelled differently, for example,
poor, **paw**, **pour**.
onset The initial consonant or consonant cluster of a word or syllable, for example, **tr**ain, **scr**ape, **sk**ate.
letter string A string of letters which remains constant in spelling, for example, **ight**.
mnemonic A system devised to aid memory, for example, I'll be your fri**END** to the **END**.
phoneme The smallest unit of sound in a word. A phoneme can be represented by one to four letters, for example,
thin, thi**ck**, thi**gh**, th**ough**.
phonics The relationship between sounds and the written form of a language.
rhyme The use of words which have the same sound in their final syllable, for example, f**ox**/r**ocks**, s**ore**/d**oor**.
rime The part of a word or syllable which contains the vowel and final consonant or consonant cluster, for example,
sh**eep**, sl**ow**, f**oal**.
syllable A rhythmic segment of a word, for example, **can** (1 syllable) , **can- op- y** (3 syllables), **tel- e- vis- ion** (4 syllables).

A word tree

Name: _____

Class: _____

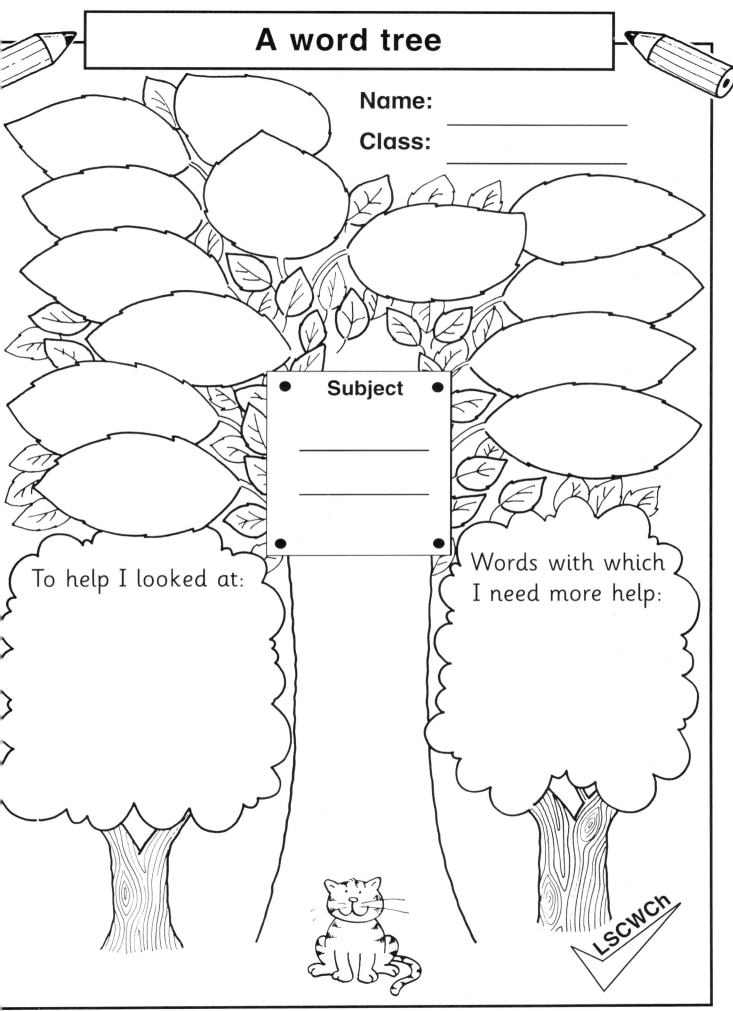

Subject

_____

_____

To help I looked at:

Words with which I need more help:

LSCWCh

Teachers' note The tree could be used in a variety of ways for different subject areas in order to make collections of words. It could also form the basis of a class display, with every child adding his or her tree to the forest. This provides an opportunity to monitor difficult spellings in different subject areas.

Developing Literacy Year 4
© A & C Black 1998

Building words

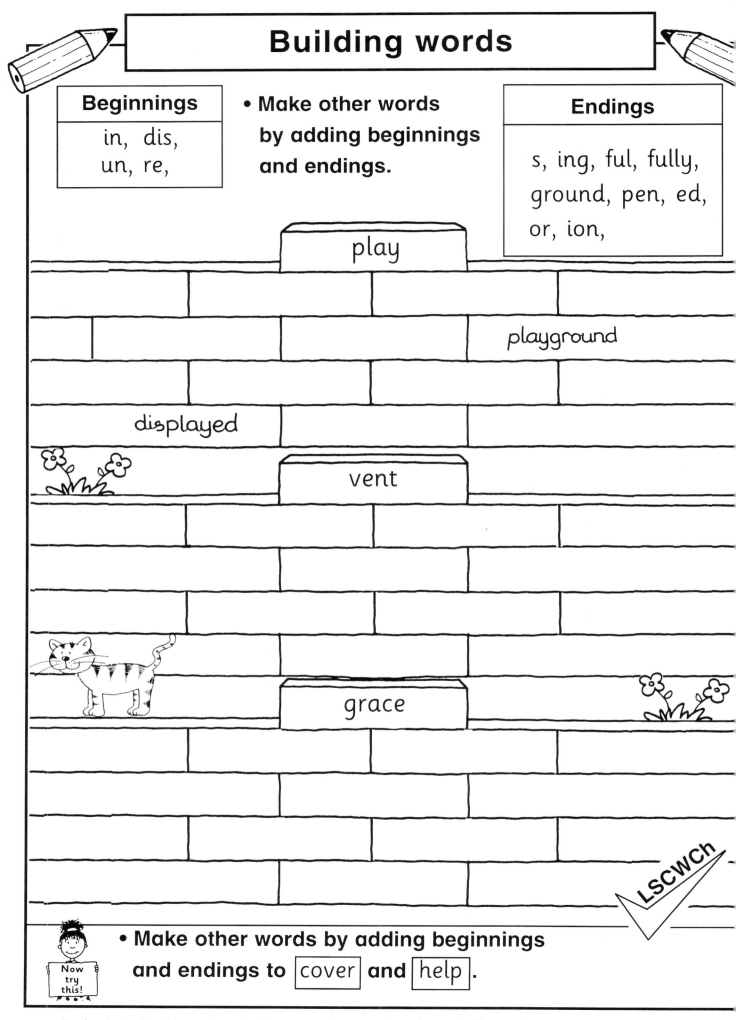

Beginnings

in, dis, un, re,

• Make other words by adding beginnings and endings.

Endings

s, ing, ful, fully, ground, pen, ed, or, ion,

play

playground

displayed

vent

grace

• Make other words by adding beginnings and endings to [cover] and [help].

Now try this!

LSCWCh

Teachers' note Use this page to revise the concepts of root words, prefixes and suffixes. During shared reading highlight words such as **invention** and ask children to identify the root word (vent). Other beginnings and endings are possible, for example, **eventful**.

Developing Literacy Year 4
© A & C Black 1998

10

Spelling with your hands

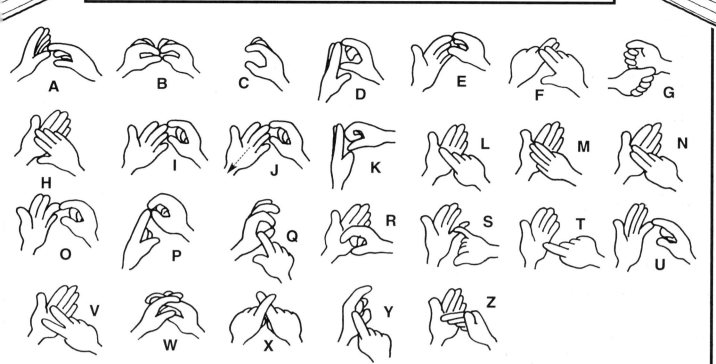

- **What do the following hand-signs spell?**
- **Write the words.**

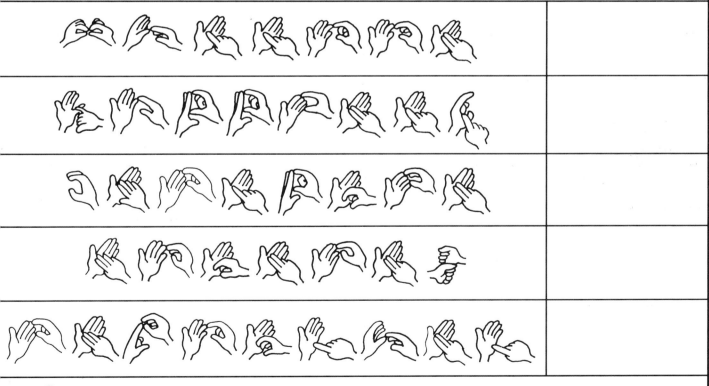

- **Draw or trace the signs to spell your name.**
- **Use sign language to write or sign a message for a partner to read.**

Now try this!

Teachers' note* This activity can be developed by asking the children to invent or use their own codes. This work should be closely linked with work on alphabetical order and dictionary work.

Developing Literacy Year 4
© A & C Black 1998

Police spelling

A	Alpha	AL-FAH		N	November	NO-VEM-BER
B	Bravo	BRAH-VOH		O	Oscar	OSS-CAH
C	Charlie	CHAR-LEE		P	Papa	PAH-PAH
D	Delta	DELL-TAH		Q	Quebec	KWE-BECK
E	Echo	ECK-OH		R	Romeo	ROW-ME-OH
F	Foxtrot	FOKS-TROT		S	Sierra	SEE-AIR-RAH
G	Golf	GOLF		T	Tango	TANG-GO
H	Hotel	HOH-TELL		U	Uniform	YOU-NEE-FORM
I	India	IN-DEE-AH		V	Victor	VIK-TAH
J	Juliet	JEW-LEE-ETT		W	Whisky	WISS-KEY
K	Kilo	KEY-LOH		X	X-ray	ECKS-RAY
L	Lima	LEE-MAH		Y	Yankee	YANG-KEY
M	Mike	MIKE		Z	Zulu	ZOO-LOO

- **Write the messages on the police cars.**

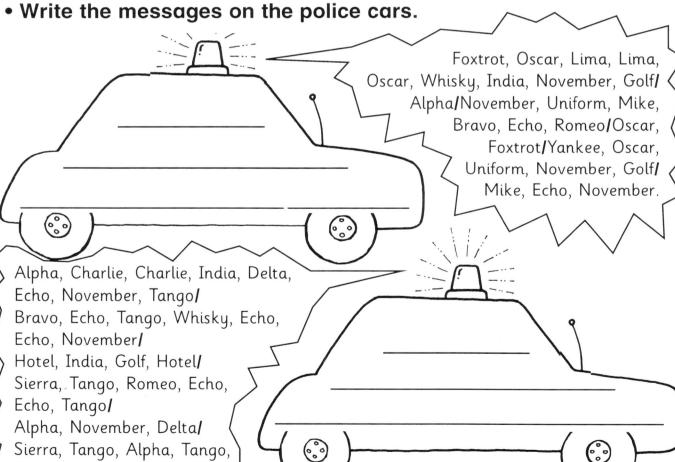

Foxtrot, Oscar, Lima, Lima, Oscar, Whisky, India, November, Golf/ Alpha/November, Uniform, Mike, Bravo, Echo, Romeo/Oscar, Foxtrot/Yankee, Oscar, Uniform, November, Golf/ Mike, Echo, November.

Alpha, Charlie, Charlie, India, Delta, Echo, November, Tango/ Bravo, Echo, Tango, Whisky, Echo, Echo, November/ Hotel, India, Golf, Hotel/ Sierra, Tango, Romeo, Echo, Echo, Tango/ Alpha, November, Delta/ Sierra, Tango, Alpha, Tango, India, Oscar, November.

- **Write a clue to tell a partner where to find some stolen goods.**

Now try this!

Teachers' note* This fun activity can be extended into class activities during which the children can try to speak in 'police spelling'. What problems do they find? Is it a good way to communicate? Why do the police use this alphabet?

Developing Literacy Year 4
© A & C Black 1998

Telephone numbers

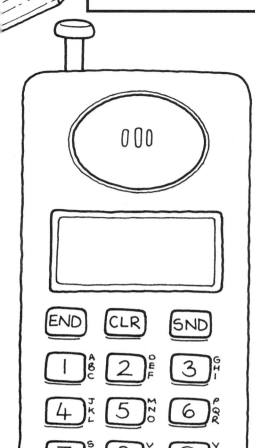

- **Use the numbers on the telephone to spell words. Read the clues first.**

Clue: The day after yesterday.

7	5	2	1	9
t	o	d	a	y

Clue: Circular.

6	5	7	5	2
r				

Clue: Every now and again.

7	5	5	2	7	3	5	2	7
s				t				s

Some people have special phone numbers.

The numbers tell other people where they work.

- **'Spell' these phone numbers.**

395 = g y m

1154 = b _ _ k

4316169 = l _ _ _ _ _ r _

35763714 = h _ _ p _ _ _ l

1366567 = a _ _ _ _ _ t

2257377 = d _ _ _ _ _ t

- **Write five names in numbers and ask a partner to spell them in letters.**

Teachers' note* Discuss the fact that in a word two numbers may be the same but may represent different letters, for example, in **round**, 65752, **5** represents first **o** and then **n**. Children could work in pairs of different abilities and discuss the possible letter combinations.

Developing Literacy Year 4
© A & C Black 1998

Words within words

- Find shorter words or names in the longer words. Your targets are given to you.

fantastic → (**4 words**)

fan an ant   as

important → (**5 words**)

_____

teacher → (**6 words**)

_____

introduction → (**5 words**)

_____

Christopher → (**7 words**)

_____

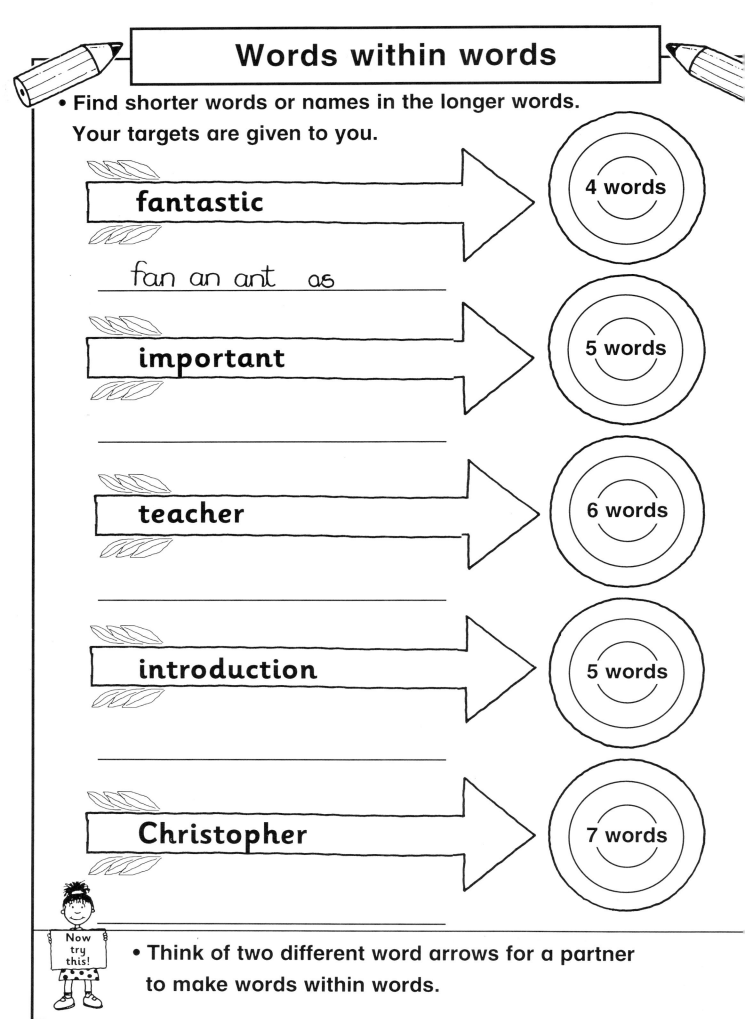

Now try this!

- Think of two different word arrows for a partner to make words within words.

Teachers' note* Ensure the children understand that the order of the letters cannot change. A display could be made with the children's own arrows. Who can find the most words from a single word?

Developing Literacy Year 4
© A & C Black 1998

Food words

- **Find the words whose letters are hidden in these food words.**
- **Write them on the food shapes.**
- **In the circles write the number of words you have made.**

bean ②

be

an

carrot

potato

chocolate

coffee

pineapple

restaurant

Menu

Now try this!

- **List the words you can find in** scrambled .
- **How many did you find?**

Use a dictionary.

Teachers' note Finding words within words is an important part of children's awareness of word-building. ...also shows them that different letter combinations can create different sound patterns, for example, be, ...n and **bean**. Ensure that children understand that they cannot change the order of the letters.

Developing Literacy Year 4
© A & C Black 1998

15

Record breaker

Fact file

Someone made 70 words from

spaghetti

by using the letters in any order.

• **How many words can you make?** _____

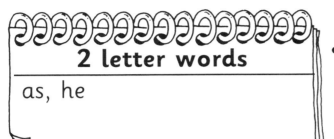

2 letter words

as, he

• **Add three other 2 letter words to the list.**

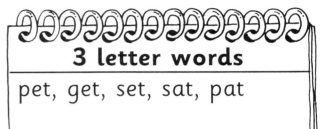

3 letter words

pet, get, set, sat, pat

• **Add ten other 3 letter words to the list.**

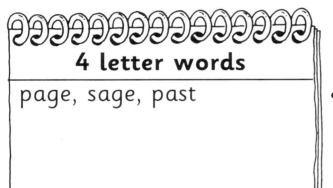

4 letter words

page, sage, past

• **Add five other 4 letter words to the list.**

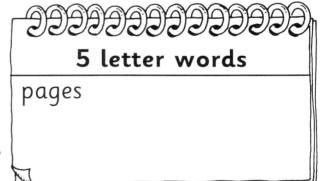

5 letter words

pages

• **Add four other 5 letter words to the list.**

• **Write as many words as you can.**
  Total number of words _____ .

Now try this!

• **Can you make a 6 letter word from** spaghetti **?**

  h _ _ _ _ _

• **How many words can you make from these?**

  hospitals (65)   telephone (38)

  The world records are in brackets.

Teachers' note* Ensure that the children understand that they can use the letters in any order. A special class word wall could be created to enable the children to spend any spare moments adding words to the list.

Developing Literacy Year 4
© A & C Black 1998

Animal anagrams

- Which animals' names do these anagrams make?
- Match them to the picture. Write the word.

shif

chicnke

fish

_____

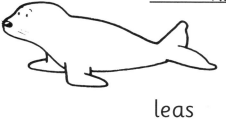

leas

giret

_____

_____

yonkem

titenk

_____

_____

tenahelp

ragfife

_____

_____

lopedat

yuppp

_____

_____

Now try this!

- **Make up some animal anagrams for a partner to solve.**
- **Use the animals' names to make an animal wordsearch for your partner to solve.**

achers' note* Anagrams are useful in developing children's awareness of the structure of words. ey could produce 'anagram books' for other topics and subjects.

Developing Literacy Year 4
© A & C Black 1998

Word robots

- **Rearrange the letters to make two anagrams for each word.**
- **Write them on the robots.**

- **Write the anagrams you can find for each of these words.**

| steal | spot | smile |

Teachers' note* During the introduction, model the first anagram. Demonstrate that the same letters in different combinations can make different sound for example, **i** and **e** in live and evil.

Developing Literacy Year 4
© A & C Black 1998

Lemons and melons

• **Change the letters around to make an anagram.**
The pictures will help.

lemon
melon

pests

mile

shrub

rats

petal

vowels

words

calm

palm

Now
try
this!

• **Find anagrams for these words:**

taps	was	dice	peach	canoe

Teachers' note* During the introduction, demonstrate a few examples of anagrams. Encourage the children to cross off each letter as they use it.

Developing Literacy Year 4
© A & C Black 1998

Word magic

- **Change one letter in each word to make a new word.**
- **Circle the letter which you have changed.**
- **Complete the ladders.**

sun

(b)un

bu(t)

(h)ut

h(o)t

mat

rug

him

her

warm

cold

ship

boat

cat

dog

rat

Now try this!

- **Can you change** hand **to** foot **?**
  It should take five steps on a ladder.
- **Make a ladder with a starting word and a finishing word for a partner to solve.**

Teachers' note* Model the first example with the children. You could adapt this sheet to make it easier for some children by writing in one or two of the words.

Developing Literacy Year 4
© A & C Black 1998

Magic mirror

The mirror turns the words back to front

- **Write the word in the picture.**
- **Write the new word.**

	Magic mirror	New word

tap   _pat_

_____   _____

_____   _____

_____   _____

_____   _____

_____   _____

_____   _____

_____   _____

Use a dictionary.

Now try this!

- **Write each new word in its own sentence.**
- **Think of three other magic mirror words for a partner.**

achers' note This is quite a 'magic' concept for children - the same letters of a word written in a
fferent order can produce a completely different word. Point out to the children that the vowel
und may change, for example, in the words star and rats.

Developing Literacy Year 4
© A & C Black 1998

21

Dictionary pages 1

- **Write the words in alphabetical order on the correct dictionary page.**

Look at the first letter, then the second letter, then the third letter.

kerb   jigsaw
          lemon
live
          key
jersey   jingle

karate   ladybird

jaw   kidney

jealous
          kick
kayak
          label
leaves

little   javelin

j   javelin
    jaw

k

l

LSCWCh

Now try this!

- **Now add these words in alphabetical order to the dictionary pages:**

  knock   loom   Judaism

  loose   judge   knowledge

- **Write each of these words in its own sentence.**

Teachers' note Encourage the children to look up in a dictionary any words they do not know. The activities focus on alphabetical order to three or four letters. A similar format could be used with children who have difficulty using a dictionary, initially asking them to identify the first letter only.

Developing Literacy Year 4
© A & C Black 1998

Dictionary pages 2

- **Write the words in alphabetical order on the correct dictionary page.**

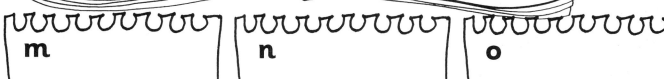

match muscle

November ordeal

outstanding outlaw

museum novice

ordinary nourish

noun

material

order

mushroom

novel

outing

nought

mattress

Look at the first letter, then the second letter, then the third letter, then the fourth letter.

m

n

o

LSCWCh

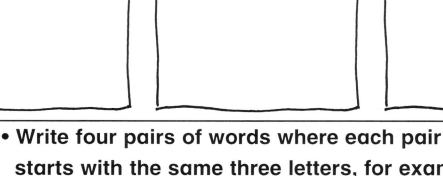

- **Write four pairs of words where each pair starts with the same three letters, for example,** valuable **and** valley .
- **Give them to a partner to put in the correct alphabetical order.**

achers' note Encourage the children to look up in the dictionary any words they do not know. uring the plenary session you could ask the meaning of 'novice' and 'ordeal' to check that they e doing this. The words focus on alphabetical order to four letters.

Developing Literacy Year 4
© A & C Black 1998

Number words

The number computer has broken down. All the words have come out at once.

- **Write the numbers which match the words.**

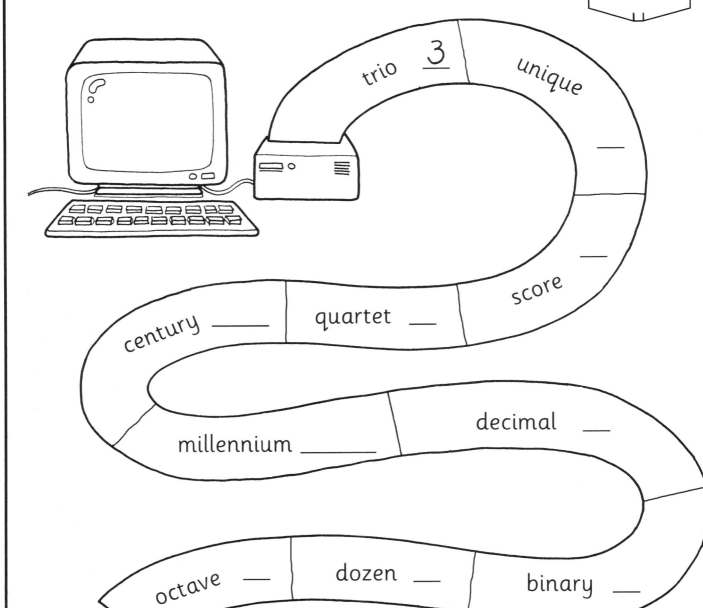

Use a dictionary

trio _3_

unique ___

score ___

century ___

quartet ___

millennium _____

decimal ___

octave ___

dozen ___

binary ___

LSCWCh

Now try this!

- **List the prefixes which tell you the number, for example, tri = 3.**
- **Use your dictionary to find ten other words which use these prefixes. Write their meanings.**

Teachers' note This sheet is a good introduction to prefixes and word derivation (although score and dozen do not have obvious prefixes). **Bi** and **tri** are useful words to start with as the children will be able to generate words using the same prefix. Ask if they know another prefix for four (**quad**).

Developing Literacy Year 4
© A & C Black 1998

Funny alphabets quiz

- The answers to the clues are letters of the alphabet. The picture clues on the page will help.
- Write the letter in the box. Write the whole word on the line.

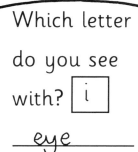

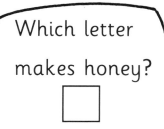

Which letter do you see with? [i]

___eye___

Which letter makes honey? [ ]

_____

Which letter is a hot drink? [ ]

_____

Which letter is a line of people waiting for a bus? [ ]

_____

Which letter is a green vegetable? [ ]

_____

Which two letters are half of 160? [ ]

_____

Which two letters are a green climbing plant? [ ]

_____

Which two letters mean freezing? [ ]

_____

Now try this!

- **What does this message say? Write it in full.**

  YY UR, YY UB, IC UR YY 4 ME.

- **Use 'funny alphabets' to write your own message for a partner.**

Teachers' note This activity gives you an opportunity to revise the alphabet, vowels and consonants. It is also a good introduction to the phonological awareness activities in the next section.

Developing Literacy Year 4
© A & C Black 1998

Difficult words

Here are some words which are difficult to spell.

- **Use the letters in the stars to complete the words.**

Use a dictionary.

w _ _ ch

p _ _ ple.

fr _ _ nd.

w _ _ er.

m _ _ ey.

y _ _ ng

w _ _ ld

s _ _ ool

th _ _ r

 at

 ou

it

 on

eo

 ie

ou

 ch

ei

witch

- **Write each word in a sentence.**

LSCWCh

 **Now try this!**

- **Write mnemonics to remember the spellings of four of the words above, for example,**

The girls and their friends.

Teachers' note These high frequency irregular words are difficult to teach. Practice and regular revision of the spellings, together with mnemonics, are the main strategies to use. Children could keep a personal list of their tricky words. They can cross off each word as they succeed in spelling it correctly.

Developing Literacy Year 4
© A & C Black 1998

Ugh! ☐ough☐ words

- **Read the words. Underline the letter string which they all have.**

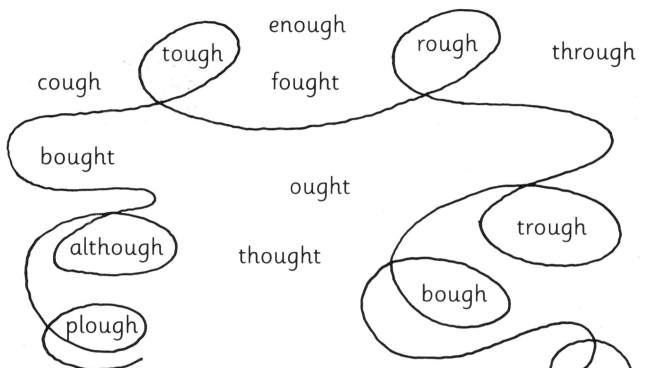

enough

tough

rough

through

cough

fought

bought

ought

trough

although

thought

bough

plough

- **Write the words in the correct lists in the chart.**
- **Complete the four 'empty' lists.**
- **Which list has the most words?**

sounds like sort	sounds like stuff	sounds like do	sounds like toe	sounds like now	sounds like off
fought	rough				

Now try this!

- **List all the** ☐ough☐ **words in alphabetical order.**
- **Choose six unusual words from the list and write a sentence showing what each word means.**

eachers' note This is an example of a letter string which has many different sounds. The children should ractise writing the letter strings to encourage the flowing cursive style and to reinforce the relationship f the letters **ough**.

Developing Literacy Year 4
© A & C Black 1998

Letter strings are and and

The words in the pens contain the letter strings are and and.

- Choose letters from the ink puddle to make new words.
  Write the words on the lines.

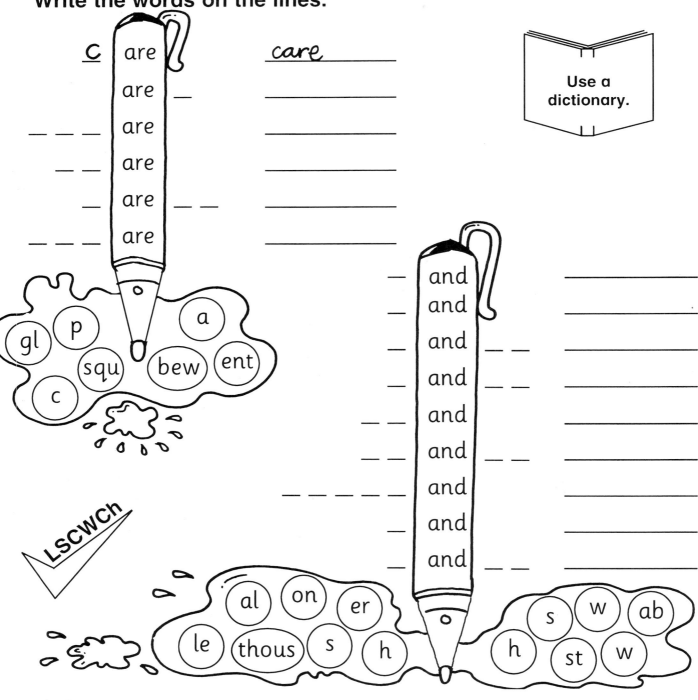

C | are — care

___ are — ___

_ _ _ are — ___

_ _ are — ___

_ are _ _ — ___

___ are — ___

Use a dictionary.

— and ___

— and ___

— and _ _ ___

— and _ _ ___

_ _ and ___

_ _ and ___

_ _ _ _ _ and ___

— and ___

— and _ _ ___

LSCWCh

Developing Literacy Year 4
© A & C Black 1998

Now try this!

- Find four other words for each of the letter strings.
- Make another pen and ink puddle for a partner, using another letter string.

Teachers' note During the whole class introduction, choose a few letter strings with which to experiment. This is the first stage in the identification of letter strings in words. It can be reinforced in handwriting practice.

• **Play 'Snap' with words and pictures.**

count

crouch

found

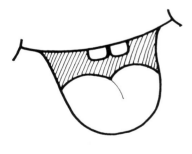

ground

loud

shout

eachers' note Pages 29-32 form a flexible resource which can be used in a variety of ways after the honemes have been introduced. These could include: a) use one letter string for each sound (phoneme), or example, **ou** and **aw**; children could play 'Snap the same sound' with just words, just pictures or vords and pictures; b) use both letter strings for each sound (phoneme) to play 'Snap the same sound'.

Developing Literacy Year 4
© **A & C Black 1998**

ow

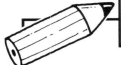

• **Play 'Snap' with words and pictures.**

brown		growl
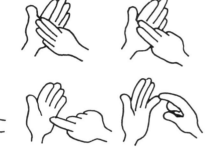	how	
now		gown
	drown	

Teachers' note Pages 29-32 form a flexible resource which can be used in a variety of ways after the phonemes have been introduced. These could include: a) use one letter string for each sound (phoneme), for example, **ou** and **aw**; children could play 'Snap the same sound' with just words, just pictures or words and pictures; b) use both letter strings for each sound (phoneme) to play 'Snap the same sound'.

Developing Literacy Year 4
© A & C Black 1998

or

- **Play 'Snap' with words and pictures.**

	before	
more		sorting
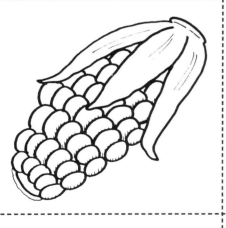	worn	
lord		snort

Teachers' note Pages 29-32 form a flexible resource which can be used in a variety of ways after the phonemes have been introduced. These could include: a) use one letter string for each sound (phoneme), for example, **ou** and **aw**; children could play 'Snap the same sound' with just words, just pictures or words and pictures; b) use both letter strings for each sound (phoneme) to play 'Snap the same sound'.

Developing Literacy Year 4
© **A & C Black 1998**

• **Play 'Snap' with words and pictures.**

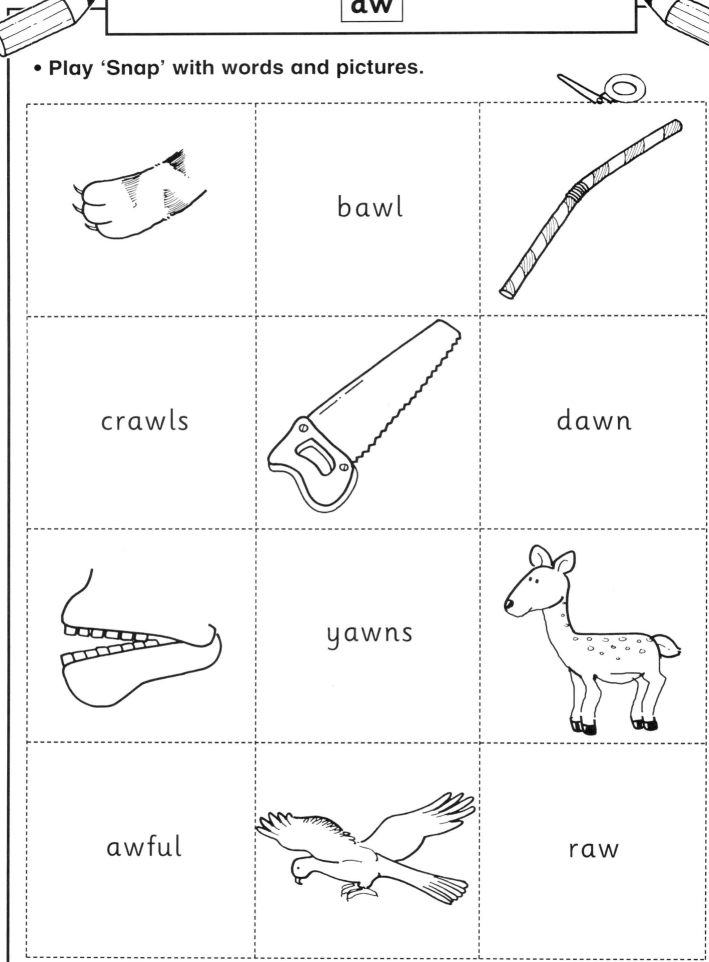

bawl

crawls

dawn

yawns

awful

raw

Teachers' note Pages 29-32 are a flexible resource which can be used in a variety of ways after the phonemes have been introduced. These could include: a) use one letter string for each sound (phoneme), for example, **ou** and **aw**; children could play 'Snap the same sound' with just words, just pictures or words and pictures; b) use both letter strings for each sound (phoneme) to play 'Snap the same sound'.

Developing Literacy Year 4
© A & C Black 1998

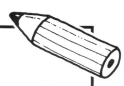

| er | ir | or | ur |

These words have the same second sound (phoneme).

- **Read the words. Circle the second sound.**

t(ur)n   herd   first   worm

- **Write the words on the correct notepads.**
- **On each notepad write at least three other words with the same sound.**

ur

fur

er

term

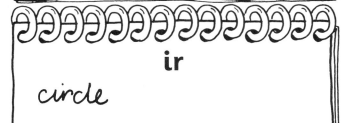

ir

circle

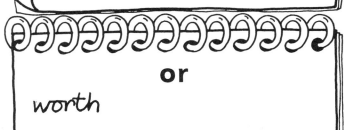

or

worth

Now try this!

- **Write all the words from the notepads in alphabetical order in one long list.**
- **Use as many words from the notepads as you can to make a long nonsense sentence, for example,**

The furry worm turned a circle.

Teachers' note Display the children's nonsense sentences to provide a word bank and assistance for those working independently. During the next shared reading session, ask the children to point out words which could have been written on the notepads.

Developing Literacy Year 4
© A & C Black 1998

Second phoneme relay

All the words in a lane must have the same second sound (phoneme).

• Help each swimmer pick up the correct word.

Write the words from the pool in the correct swimmer's lane.

sounds like too

sounds like would

sounds like pain

sounds like burn

two

fade

word pool

through   wood   world   stood   turn

pail   fern   flew   lane   true   sir   stay   ~~two~~

could   put   dirty   shoe   pay   soot   ~~fade~~

• Circle the letters which make the second sound.

• Add two other words to each lane.

Now try this!

• How many combinations of letters can you find for each lane?

• Write the answer at the bottom of the lane.

Teachers' note Regional variations in accents will provide an opportunity for discussion, for example, how do children pronounce **soot**? Does it sound like **would** or **too**? Children should understand that sounds (phonemes) can often be written using different letters (graphemes).

Developing Literacy Year 4
© A & C Black 1998

Homophones

Say the word for the picture. Write the word.
- **Write a word which sounds the same but is spelled differently.**
- **Write the meaning of the word.**

Use a
dictionary.

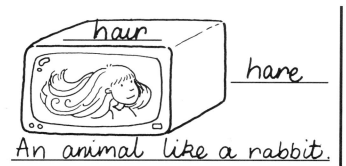

hair

hare

An animal like a rabbit.

_____

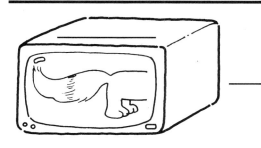

_____

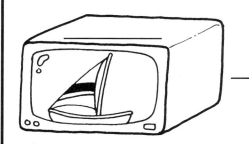

_____

_____

_____

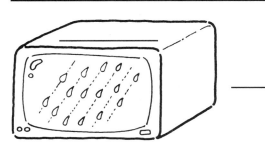

_____

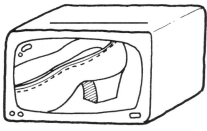

_____

Now
try
this!

To **has two homophones;** two **and** too.
- **Write two homophones with sentences**
  for poor , there **and** road .

LSCWCh

eachers' note By bringing homophones to children's attention as a peculiarity of language, they are
ore likely to be able to deal with them and learn to remember the spelling of the alternatives. Make
splays of the words and their different spellings.

Developing Literacy Year 4
© **A & C Black 1998**

Space invaders

- **Circle the letter strings** $\boxed{\text{and}}$, $\boxed{\text{as}}$ **or** $\boxed{\text{one}}$ **in these words.**

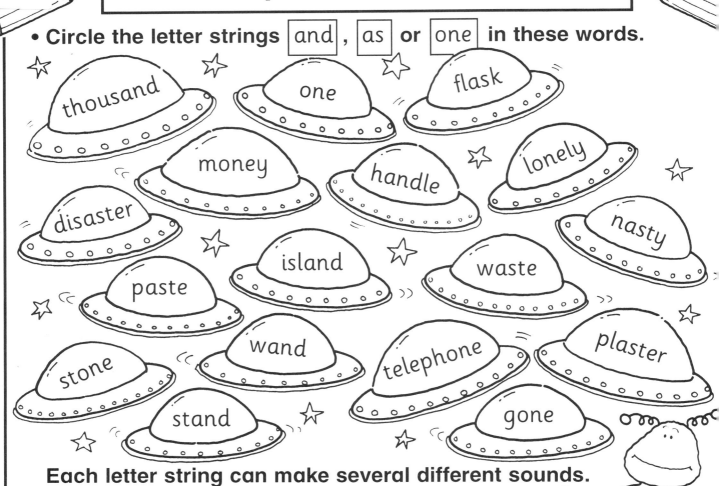

Each letter string can make several different sounds.

- **Write the words in the chart.**

sounds like					
ask	taste	hand	wander	alone	done

LSCWCh

- **Which word does not fit in to any column?** _____

- **Think of three other words for each of the letter strings** $\boxed{\text{and}}$, $\boxed{\text{as}}$ **and** $\boxed{\text{one}}$.
- **Write the new words in the correct column in the chart.**

Teachers' note Regional variations may influence the sounds of the letter strings. This could be a focus for discussion during the plenary session. The children need to investigate the letters surrounding the letter strings to try to work out under what circumstances certain sounds are made.

Developing Literacy Year 4
© A & C Black 1998

Word birds

The words in each nest have the same letter string.

- Circle that letter string.
- Which eggs do not belong in the word birds' nests?
- Read the words. Write the word which sounds different.

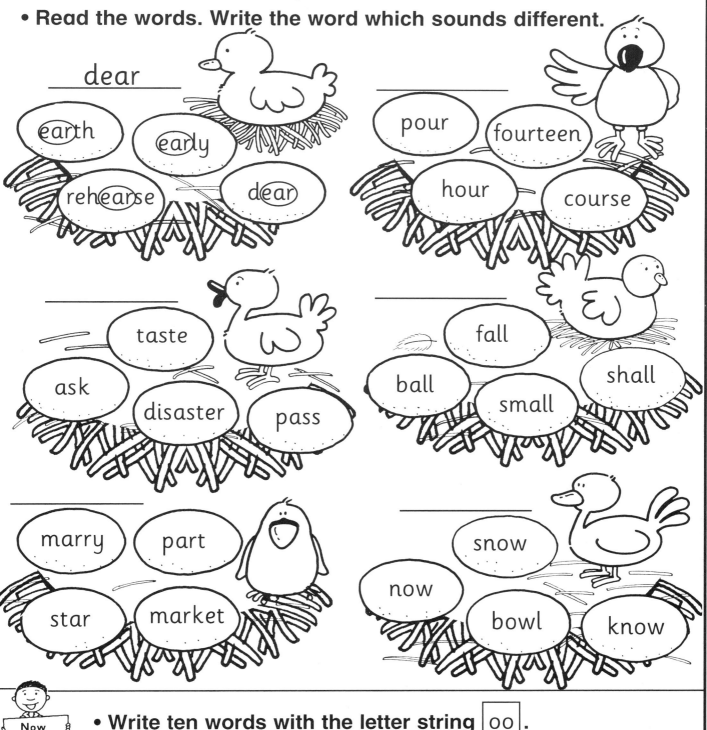

dear

earth   early   rehearse   dear

pour   fourteen   hour   course

taste   ask   disaster   pass

fall   ball   small   shall

marry   part   star   market

snow   now   bowl   know

Now try this!

- Write ten words with the letter string $\boxed{oo}$.
- List them in columns for different sounds.
- How many different sounds does $\boxed{oo}$ make?

Teachers' note It is important that the children realise that the same letter strings (graphemes) do not always make the same sounds (phonemes). This concept could be developed during the first half of the Literacy Hour, by listing words with the same letter string and several different sounds.

Developing Literacy Year 4
© A & C Black 1998

Plurals revision

- **Find all the things in the picture which end in** $\boxed{\text{ch}}$, $\boxed{\text{sh}}$ **or** $\boxed{\text{x}}$.
- **Write the words. Write their plurals.**

Singular	Plural	Singular	Plural
beach	*beaches*		

LSCWCh

Now try this!

- **Write a rule for making plurals of words ending in** $\boxed{\text{ch}}$, $\boxed{\text{sh}}$ **or** $\boxed{\text{x}}$.
- **Write six other plurals which end in** $\boxed{\text{es}}$.

Teachers' note Identify particular plural endings during shared reading sessions. Ask the children to point them out, generate new examples and write them on a display to form a class word bank. Plurals of words ending in **o** (covered in **Developing Literacy Year 3**) could also be revised.

Developing Literacy Year 4
© A & C Black 1998

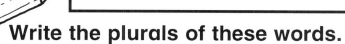

Plurals maths

Write the plurals of these words.

leaf   leaf = _leaves_   ruby   ruby = _____

knife   knife = _____   party   party = _____

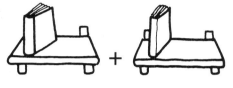   

shelf   shelf = _____   puppy   puppy = _____

wolf   wolf = _____   story   story = _____

loaf   loaf = _____   pony   pony = _____

- **Write a rule for making plurals of words ending in | f | or | fe | .**
- **Write a rule for making plurals of words ending in | y | .**

Now try this!

- **What are the plurals of these words?**

| key | | day | | boy | | monkey | | valley |

- **How are these plurals different from those in the pictures? (Hint: Look at the letter which comes before | y | .)**

'eachers' note The children should be asked to generate other examples, categorise them and develop
rule, for example, 'with a vowel before the **y**, just add **s**'. Encourage them to find exceptions, for
xample, dwar**fs**, clif**fs** and roo**fs**.

Developing Literacy Year 4
© A & C Black 1998

Strange plurals

- **Circle the correct plural for each word.**
  Write the correct plural.

Use a
dictionary.

singular: mouse

mousse, mices,
mouses, (mice)

plural: _mice_

singular: die

di, dies,
dice, dices

plural: _____

singular: dozen

dozens, dozeni,
dozen, doz

plural: _____

singular: tooth

tooths, toothen,
teeth, teeths

plural: _____

singular: man

mans, mens,
man, men

plural: _____

singular: woman

women, womans
womens, woman

plural: _____

singular: foot

foots, foot,
feets, feet

plural: _____

singular: scissors

scissori, scissors,
scissor, scissorum

plural: _____

singular: goose

gooses, gander,
geese, geeses

plural: _____

singular: wish

wishes, wish,
wishing, wit

plural: _____

- **Write the plurals of these words:**

Now
try
this!

mother-in-law _____   cactus _____

index _____   sheep _____

piano _____   child _____

Teachers' note Link the work on irregular plurals with work on language derivation, for example, 'man' and 'woman' are derived from Anglo-Saxon. The children could challenge partners to find other plurals, explaining how they reached their answer.

Developing Literacy Year 4
© A & C Black 1998

Verb endings 1

- **Look for the verb in each picture.**
  Write the verb below the picture.

1.	to *slide*	2.	to	3.	to
4.	to	5.	to	6.	to

- **What do you notice about the last letter of all these verbs?**
- **Write what the people are doing in each picture.**

1. She is sliding.   2. _____

3. _____   4. _____

5. _____   6. _____

LSCWCh

- **What happens to the spelling of these verbs when you add** `ing` **?** _____

Now try this!

- **Add** `ing` **to these verbs and write the new word:**
  share, hope, take, vote, choose, love.
- **Now write each** `ing` **word in a sentence.**

Teachers' note Many teachers have their own mnemonic for the 'drop the e' rule. This could be linked to sentence-level work on verbs, including participles and the infinitive. The focus should be on children generating more examples and formulating a rule.

Verb endings 2

• **Complete the spaces in the script for** *Cinderella*. **Use the verbs in the coach, but make sure they all end in** $\boxed{s}$.

Ideas for the script for <u>Cinderella</u>

Her sister ___envies___ her.

The Prince t _____ the slipper on her foot.

Cinderella h _____ to the ball.

The Fairy Godmother f _____ to help her out.

She e _____ the cupboard to find a pumpkin.

Prince Charming c _____ her off.

She m _____ him and c _____ in church.

She d _____ her eyes and is happy.

to dry   to marry

to try   to carry

to envy   to cry

to fly   to hurry

to empty

LSCWCh

Now try this!

• **Write sentences for five of the verbs in the coach, using the** $\boxed{s}$ **ending of the verb.**

• **What happens to the** $\boxed{y}$ **at the end of the verb?**

Teachers' note This work links with plurals (**y-ies/y-ys**) and with sentence-level work on verbs in the infinitive and the present tense. Use traditional tales to tell stories in the varying tenses and discuss changes in the spellings of verbs during the plenary session.

Developing Literacy Year 4
© A & C Black 1998

• **What are the children doing? Write the verbs in the boxes.**

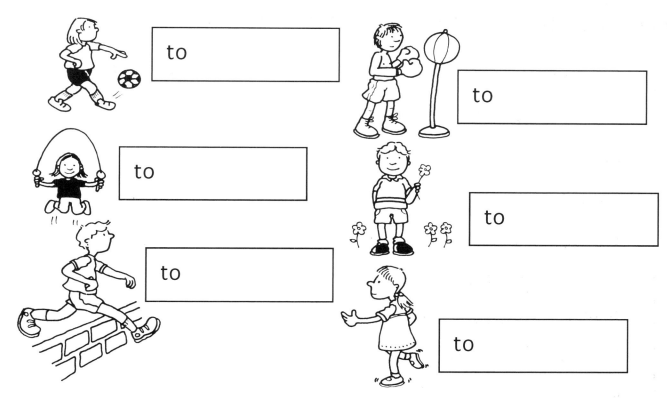

to

to

to

to

to

to

• **Add** ed **to the verbs from the pictures, for example,**

Yesterday the children ...

_____   _____   _____

_____   _____   _____

• **Which verb doubles its last letter?**

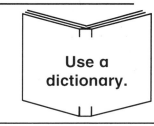

Use a dictionary.

Now try this!

• **Investigate the verbs which doubled their last letter:**

★ Is the last letter a vowel or a consonant? _____

★ Is the second-to-last letter a vowel or a consonant? _____

★ How many syllables do the verbs contain? _____

• **Write a rule about why some verbs double their last letter**

when you add ed .

Teachers' note Encourage the children to investigate word-building strategies and to develop rules or principles which will help them to become independent. Help the children to realise that single-syllable words ending in a consonant, preceded by a vowel, double their last letter if **ed** can be added.

Developing Literacy Year 4
© A & C Black 1998

43

Tense changes

- **Find the matching verbs. Write them on the notepad.**
- **On the notepad circle the letters which change.**

told

to come

had

to make

dug

to have

knew

fell

to tell

made

came

to dig

did

woke

to wake

to fall

to do

to know

to come
came

- **Here are three other verbs:**

  to sing   to blow   to drive.

- **Write three sentences for each verb, starting**

  Today I am …   Yesterday I …   Tomorrow I shall …

- **Circle the letters which change in the spelling of the verb.**

Now try this!

Teachers' note A display could be made of verbs which change their spelling (irregular verbs) with the columns 'Today I am…', 'Yesterday I …', 'Tomorrow I shall …'. Children could add more words to the columns as they come across them in their reading.

Developing Literacy Year 4
© A & C Black 1998

44

Locomot ion solut ion

- **Add** ion **to these words.**
- **Read the words.**

You might have to change the endings of some of the words.

Use a dictionary.

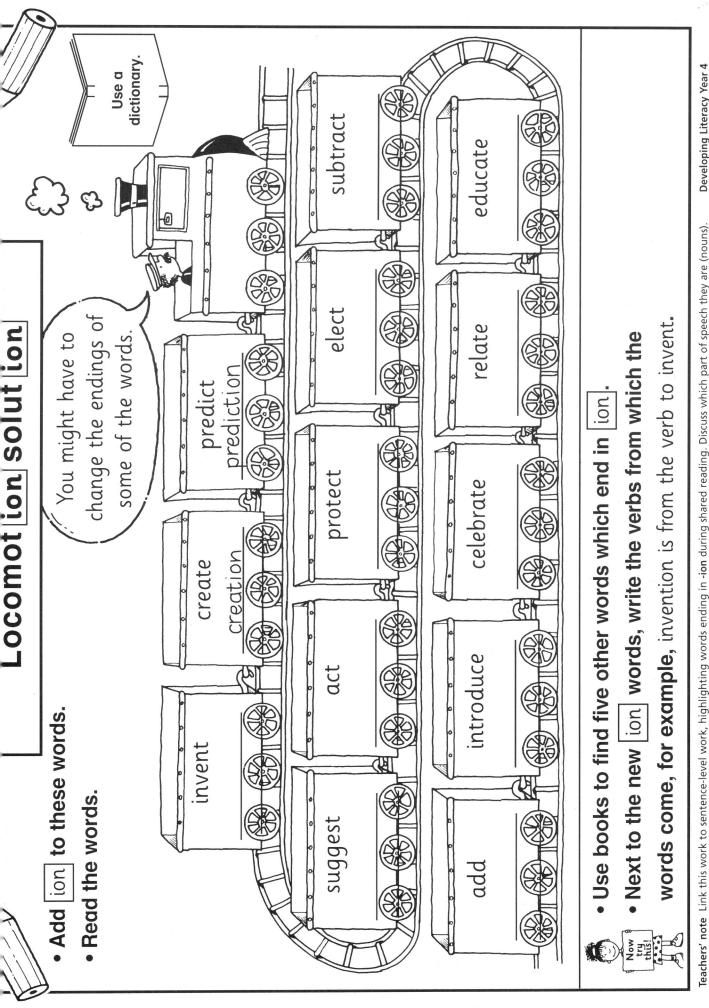

invent

create
creation

predict
prediction

suggest

act

protect

elect

subtract

add

introduce

celebrate

relate

educate

- Use books to find five other words which end in ion.
- Next to the new ion words, write the verbs from which the words come, for example, invention is from the verb to invent.

Now try this!

Teachers' note Link this work to sentence-level work, highlighting words ending in -ion during shared reading. Discuss which part of speech they are (nouns). Model with the children how to identify the root of the word: identify the verb by adding "to" in front of the word (to create). Investigate any spelling changes which take place at the end of the words, for example, dropping the final e.

Developing Literacy Year 4
© A & C Black 1998

45

Word wheel

The endings of 'special' and 'social' sound like 'shull'.

- Cut out and make the word wheel.
- Turn the wheel to make new words.
- Write the new word and show how you changed the ending before adding $\boxed{\text{ial}}$.

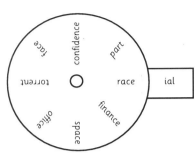

Use a dictionary.

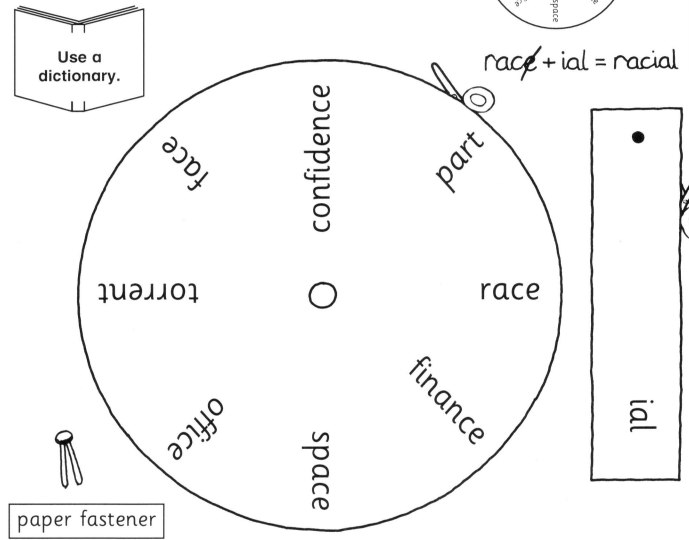

race + ial = racial

ial

paper fastener

LSCWCh

Now try this!

- **Sort the words into two columns.**

tial	cial
	racial

- **Find five other words which end in $\boxed{\text{ial}}$.**

  Add them to the correct column in your chart.

Teachers' note The children could work in pairs, competitively or co-operatively, taking turns to make a word while their partner checks it in the dictionary. 'Confiden**ce**' becomes 'confiden**tial**'; 'spa**tial**' is a more common form than 'spa**cial**'. The changes to the endings of the words when suffixes are added should be discussed in the plenary session and highlighted on word walls.

Developing Literacy Year 4
© A & C Black 1998

46

Conundrums

All these words end in |ious|.

• Sort out the letters. Write the word.

Use a dictionary.

| e | i | c | o | l | u | i | s | d |
| d | e | l | i | c | i | o | u | s |

_____

| c | i | s | o | n | u | c | s | o |

_____

| i | p | c | o | s | u | a | s |

_____

| u | i | c | o | v | i | s |

_____

| s | p | u | c | r | o | e | i |

_____

| o | r | i | g | a | s | c | u |

_____

LSCWCh

Now try this!

• **Find out what the words mean. Write them in sentences.**

• **Write three other words which end in** |ious|.

You could look for them in books.

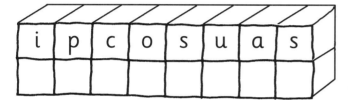

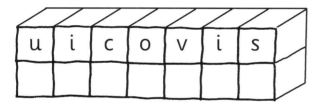

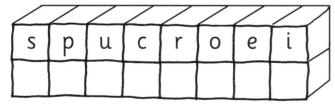

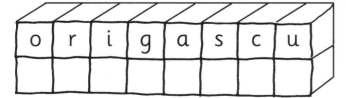

eachers' note* Link this work to the identification of such endings in shared reading and writing.
ildren could make charts for the various word endings in the 'shus' sound (tious, cious). Two useful
elling strategies are breaking the words into syllables and 'drawing' the shape of the words in boxes.

Developing Literacy Year 4
© A & C Black 1998

Syllable snakes

- Find the words in the snakes and separate them with a line.
- Divide the words into syllables with smaller lines.
- Write each word and write in brackets how many syllables it contains.

1.

importantdinnerfantasticsister

2.

beganchildrenmoneysystem

3.

uponfollowballoonbrother

1. _im/por/tant_ (3)   2. _____   3. _____

_____   _____   _____

_____   _____   _____

_____   _____   _____

- Draw two new syllable snakes.
- Fill them with two-syllable words.
- Give them to a partner to find the words and divide them into syllables.

Teachers' note Children should practise counting or tapping out the number of syllables, ensuring there is a vowel in each syllable.

Developing Literacy Year 4
© A & C Black 1998

Syllable beavers

The beavers are building word dams. They only collect words with the right number of syllables.

• Choose words from the word pool. Write them in the correct dam for 2, 3 or 4 syllables.

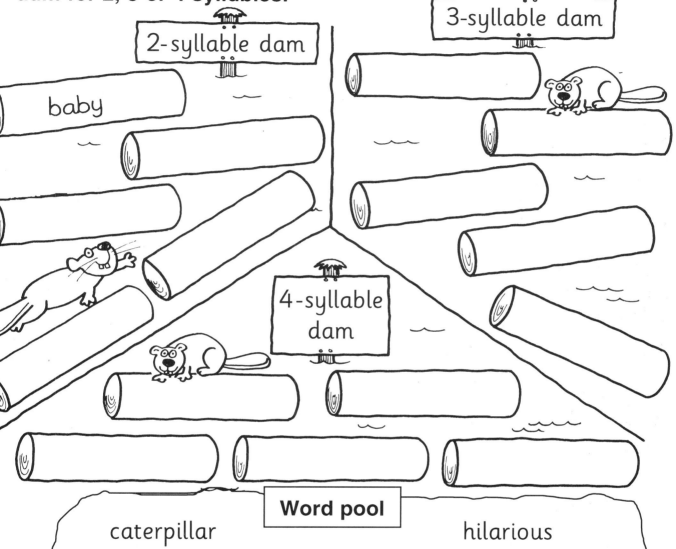

Word pool

caterpillar   hilarious

mountainous   rabbit   bicycle   community

volcano   education   ~~baby~~   monkey   apple

suddenly   dictionary   disappear   flower

LSCWCh

Now try this!

• Can you think of any 5-syllable words? Write down as many as you can.

Use a dictionary.

chers' note   You could play a game with the children in which each child has to add a word to the rect column according to the number of syllables. A display could be made of the 5-syllable words. sure that children check the meaning of the words they do not know.

Developing Literacy Year 4
© A & C Black 1998

49

Making words

- **Make words using one syllable from each box.**
- **Write the words on the lines below.**

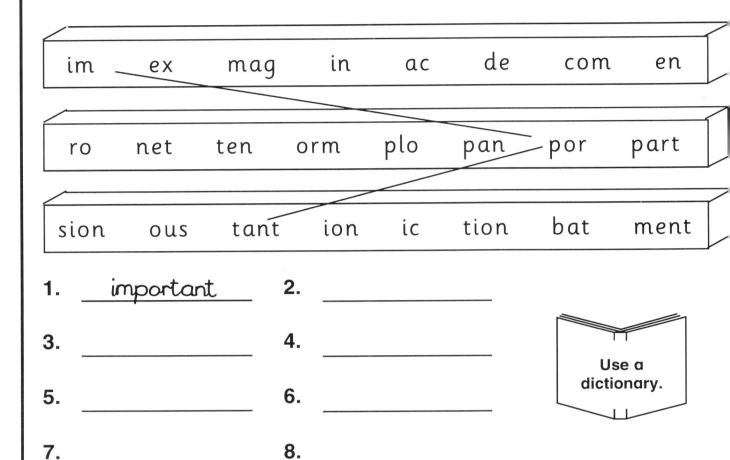

| im | ex | mag | in | ac | de | com | en |

| ro | net | ten | orm | plo | pan | por | part |

| sion | ous | tant | ion | ic | tion | bat | ment |

1. _important_   2. _____

3. _____   4. _____

5. _____   6. _____

Use a dictionary.

7. _____   8. _____

Now try this!

- **Write a long word. Cut it into syllables and mix them up.**
- **Give the mixed–up syllables to a partner to make the word. If necessary, give a clue.**

| ting | gus | dis | | dis | gus | ting |

- **Cut two long words into syllables and mix them up.**
- **Give them to a partner to solve.**

Teachers' note Introduce the activity by asking the children to clap or count the syllables in names or words. Breaking words into syllables will help the children's spelling using the building block principle. They will learn to identify and spell specific syllables, for example, 'tion'.   **Developing Literacy Year 4** © A & C Black 1998

Cockney rhyming slang

- **Join each phrase to a word which rhymes.**
- **Write the rhyming words and circle the rhyme sound.**
- **Are the rhyme sounds always spelled the same?** _____

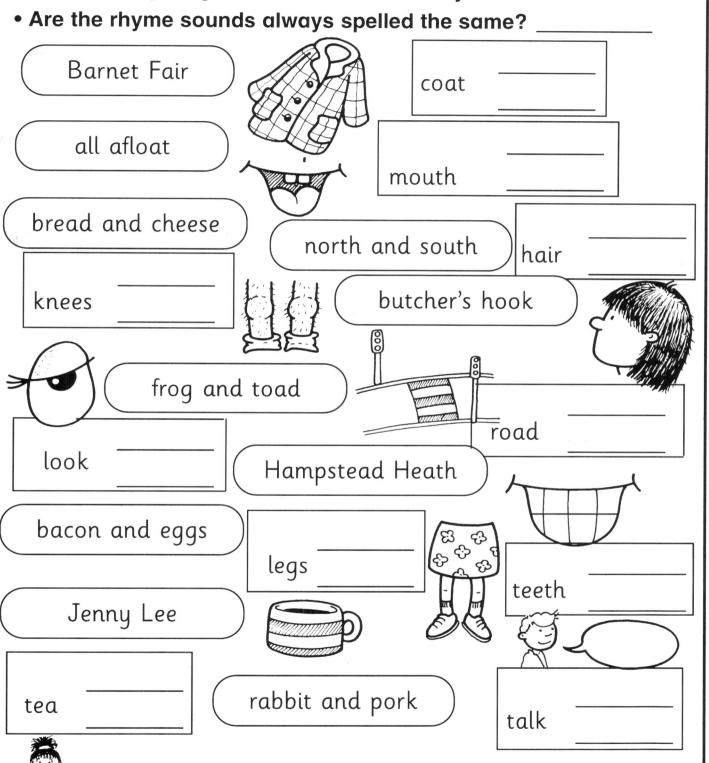

Barnet Fair

all afloat

bread and cheese

north and south

butcher's hook

frog and toad

Hampstead Heath

bacon and eggs

Jenny Lee

rabbit and pork

coat _____

mouth _____

hair _____

knees _____

look _____

road _____

legs _____

teeth _____

tea _____

talk _____

Now try this!

- **Write a message using rhyming slang.**
- **Give it to a partner to write the meaning.**

Teachers' note Introduce some examples of rhyming slang as a shared text and ask the children to guess the rhyming word. Ensure that the children understand that the rhyme sounds do not have to be made of the same letters.

Developing Literacy Year 4
© A & C Black 1998

Rhymes

- **Choose something from the picture which rhymes.**
- **Write the word. Circle the rhyme sound.**

m(ugs) of   b(ugs) _____

loads of   _____

jars of   _____

bins of   _____

box of   _____

boats of   _____

dish of   _____

pools of   _____

chests of   _____

pockets of   _____

Now try this!

- **Write the pairs of rhyming words from above which are spelled differently.**
- **Finish the rhymes in this poem:**

    Inside the magic room I saw...
    cups of _____
    packs of _____
    crates of _____
    vans of _____

- **Write two other lines.**

Teachers' note To introduce rhyme, you could play a rhyme game, for example 'In my sack, I have a back, a quack, a track …'. It is important that the children understand that the rhyme sounds can be spelled differently.

Developing Literacy Year
© A & C Black 1998

Mnemonics

Mnemonics help you to remember things.

Ⓦasps Ⓐlways Ⓢting **helps you remember how to spell** was.

• **With which words do these mnemonics help you?**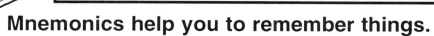

Mother ants never yell. _____

Dads often eat sugar. _____

Come on 'u' like doughnuts. _____

• **Think of a mnemonic to help you spell:**

b _____   n _____

e _____   e _____

c _____   c _____

a _____   e _____

u _____   s _____

s _____   s _____

e _____   a _____

                       r _____

                       y _____

• **Write some sentences to help you remember these words.**
  Look at the clues in the circles.

ⓅieⒺce   Have a piece of pie. _____

hⒺⓐⓡ   _____

friⒺnⒹ   _____

wⒽⓐⓣ   _____

• **How would you help a friend to spell these two words?**

    island   separate

• **Can you find any words inside them to help?**

Teachers' note Writing acrostics using children's names is a good way of introducing these activities. The class could try and think of mnemonics for words they find difficult. In the extension activity, the children might recognise **land** in **island** and **rat** in **separate**.

Developing Literacy Year 4
© **A & C Black 1998**

'Nice' words

Here are some more interesting words for 'nice'.

- **Work out the clues. Write the words.**

a nice day: f _ _ _

a nice policeman: k _ _ _

a nice holiday: w _ _ d _ _ _ _ l

a nice person: fr _ _ n _ _ y

a nice talk: i _ _ _ _ _ s _ _ _ g

a nice drink: r e _ _ _ sh _ _ g

a nice dress: p _ _ _ _ y

a nice surprise: pl _ _ s _ _ t

a nice jacket: f _ sh _ _ _ _ _ le

a nice party: en _ _ y _ _ l e

- **Now find the words in this wordsearch and circle them.**

o	k	i	n	d	e	q	m	a	o	l	b	e	r
a	x	t	a	b	n	p	l	e	a	s	a	n	t
i	w	c	u	f	i	n	e	j	v	u	m	j	d
n	w	o	n	d	e	r	f	u	l	t	g	o	i
t	j	l	s	u	e	w	r	y	z	e	i	y	f
e	k	c	w	o	k	o	i	o	m	q	y	a	e
r	o	y	k	t	d	w	e	d	a	l	r	b	b
e	t	b	w	o	e	t	n	h	y	b	m	l	t
s	t	o	a	e	l	j	d	e	r	a	z	e	e
t	h	z	m	a	w	h	l	s	o	t	i	t	o
i	y	p	r	e	t	t	y	r	y	w	o	g	l
n	p	j	f	a	s	h	i	o	n	a	b	l	e
g	d	a	v	i	y	s	u	r	z	r	p	x	u
w	r	e	f	r	e	s	h	i	n	g	e	j	w

Nice!

- **Find five other interesting words for 'nice'.**

  Use them in sentences.

- **Make your own 'nice' wordsearch and test a partner.**

Now try this!

LSCWCh

Teachers' note You could develop work from previous years by making synonym and antonym games. During the introduction to this lesson, discuss effective use of vocabulary with examples from shared and guided reading, especially in poetry.

Developing Literacy Year 4
© A & C Black 1998

'Said' words

These ten words are all more interesting words to use than 'said'.

Use a dictionary.

muttered   moaned   hissed

shrieked   demanded   snarled   mumbled

screamed   groaned   yelled

The words below are muddled up.

• **Write them correctly.**

1. ongrade: _groaned_
2. kidreesh: _____
3. dddeeanm: _____
4. dummleb: _____
5. dreamsec: _____

6. oaemnd: _____
7. ssideh: _____
8. lednars: _____
9. delley: _____
10. ttmeerdu: _____

• **Now write each word in the correct speech bubble.**

Said something loudly	Said something angrily	Said something quietly

Now try this!

• **Use a thesaurus to find four other words for 'said'.**
• **Use each word in a sentence to show that you understand its meaning.**
• **Mix up the letters of your four words and give them to a partner to solve.**

LSCWCh

Teachers' note A display could be made to record new and interesting words on the class word wall. This will provide a bank of useful words from which to develop writing activities.

Developing Literacy Year 4
© A & C Black 1998

55

'Big' words

- **With a partner, write down as many words as you can which mean 'big'.**

Use a dictionary.

enormous, towering _____

_____

_____

Here are eight words which all mean 'big' but the letters are muddled up.

LSCWCh

- **Write them out correctly by the side.**

1. scupiaso: s _ _ c _ _ _ s

2. vamssei: m _ _ s _ _ e

3. vats: v _ _ _

4. ismemen: i _ m _ _ _ e

5. citggian: g _ _ _ _ t _ c

6. egintrow: t _ w _ _ _ _ g

7. oorusenm: e _ _ r _ _ _ s

8. grate: g _ _ _ _

- **Write the words which you think best describe these three 'big' things:**

the _____ monster

the _____ continent

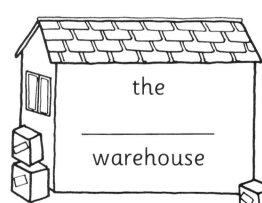

the _____ warehouse

Now try this!

- **Use four other interesting 'big' words in sentences to show their meanings.**
- **Hide your four 'big' words in a wordsearch.**
- **Give it to a partner to find the words.**

LSCWCh

Teachers' note Ask the children to brainstorm words for 'big', ensuring that the words in the anagrams are mentioned. Discuss why some words might be more appropriate than others, for example, 'towering' would be good to describe a rocket or a block of flats.

Developing Literacy Year 4
© A & C Black 1998

'Hot' words

The computer dictionary and thesaurus have broken down.

- Choose ten of the words below meaning 'hot'.
  Write their meanings.

Use a dictionary.

> tropical, humid, muggy, steamy, sticky, stifling, sunny, spicy, burning, baking, blistering, boiling, fiery, scalding, scorching, | sizzling | , sultry, sweltering, torrid.

Word	Meaning
sizzling	hissing sound when frying or burning.

LSCWCh ✓

Now try this!

- Look up 'cold' in your thesaurus. List the words you find which mean the same.
- Use five of them in sentences to show that you understand what they mean.

Teachers' note Ask the children to rewrite the list, starting with what they think is the 'hottest' word
...ing down to the word which is 'least hot'. This would provide an interesting topic for discussion during
...e plenary session.

Developing Literacy Year 4
© A & C Black 1998

Verb wordsearch

- **Circle these verbs in the wordsearch.**

asked	does	opened	used	coming
began	heard	stopped	write	knew
brought	jumped	thought	tries	

t	h	o	u	g	h	t	b	m	g
s	h	u	y	a	h	e	a	r	d
t	b	r	o	u	g	h	t	v	o
o	w	r	i	t	e	w	c	f	e
p	l	a	s	k	e	d	e	g	s
p	x	t	j	s	j	d	n	k	d
e	k	n	e	w	u	i	e	b	l
d	s	i	c	r	m	u	s	e	d
z	r	b	f	o	p	q	m	g	h
t	a	g	c	i	e	p	j	a	n
o	p	e	n	e	d	l	o	n	k

LSCWCh ✓

Now try this!

- **Write all the verbs from the wordsearch using**

$\boxed{\text{to _____}}$ **, for example:**

knew - to know

Teachers' note The verbs in the wordsearch were chosen to show the variety of verb forms, for example, past tense, present participle. This work can be of use in sentence-level work and reference should be made to it in shared and guided reading.

Developing Literacy Year 4
© A & C Black 1998

Time wordsearch

• **Circle these 'time' words in the word search.**

almost	always	young	now	during
every	number	often	sometimes	suddenly
today	until	upon	while	year

y	e	a	r	d	u	r	i	n	g
e	v	e	r	y	t	o	d	a	y
a	h	m	i	n	u	m	b	e	r
n	a	s	u	d	d	e	n	l	y
a	l	m	o	s	t	j	n	o	w
w	w	k	b	o	t	u	p	o	n
h	a	n	e	w	u	n	e	f	l
i	y	o	u	n	g	t	d	t	q
l	s	o	m	e	t	i	m	e	s
e	w	f	r	l	v	l	s	n	e

LSCWCh

Now try this!

• **Turn over this sheet. Ask a partner to read the words aloud for you to write.**
• **Make a wordsearch for a partner, including ten words to do with the seasons, the school year and clocks.**

---

achers' note Display the words in the classroom. The children can refer to these time words during ared and guided reading.

Developing Literacy Year 4
© A & C Black 1998

Position and direction wordsearch

- Circle ten 'position' or 'direction' words in this wordsearch.
- Write the words on the notepad.

a	c	r	o	s	s	m	b	y	t
b	v	g	n	e	a	r	e	n	h
e	b	o	x	f	b	l	t	b	r
h	e	a	o	p	o	e	w	e	o
i	l	l	u	k	v	d	e	s	u
n	o	o	t	r	e	q	e	i	g
d	w	n	s	c	r	s	n	d	h
h	a	g	i	n	s	i	d	e	b
a	l	t	d	a	r	o	u	n	d
u	n	d	e	r	b	z	u	w	a

across

LSCWCh

Now try this!

- Write the words which best describe the position of the alien.

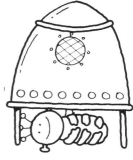

_____ _____ _____

Teachers' note Encourage the children to look up any words they do not understand in a dictionary. 'Specialist' word banks can be written on to wall displays for use during shared and guided reading.

Developing Literacy Year 4
© A & C Black 1998

Compound word flowers

- **Write words on the petals to make compound words.**
- **List the compound words.**

man

snow

flake

snowflake
snowman

sun

foot

some

Now try this!

- **Make other compound word flowers using** news **,** house **and** school **.**

Teachers' note This requires the children to think of words in 'chunks'. If they can spell one part of the word, it becomes easier for them to extend and develop their spelling knowledge. The flower idea could be used as a class display with the children adding new words as they discover them.

Developing Literacy Year 4
© A & C Black 1998

61

Inventing new words machine

- **Use the word machine to invent new words.**
- **Write what you think each word means.**
- **Tick any words which exist in a dictionary.**

Use a dictionary.

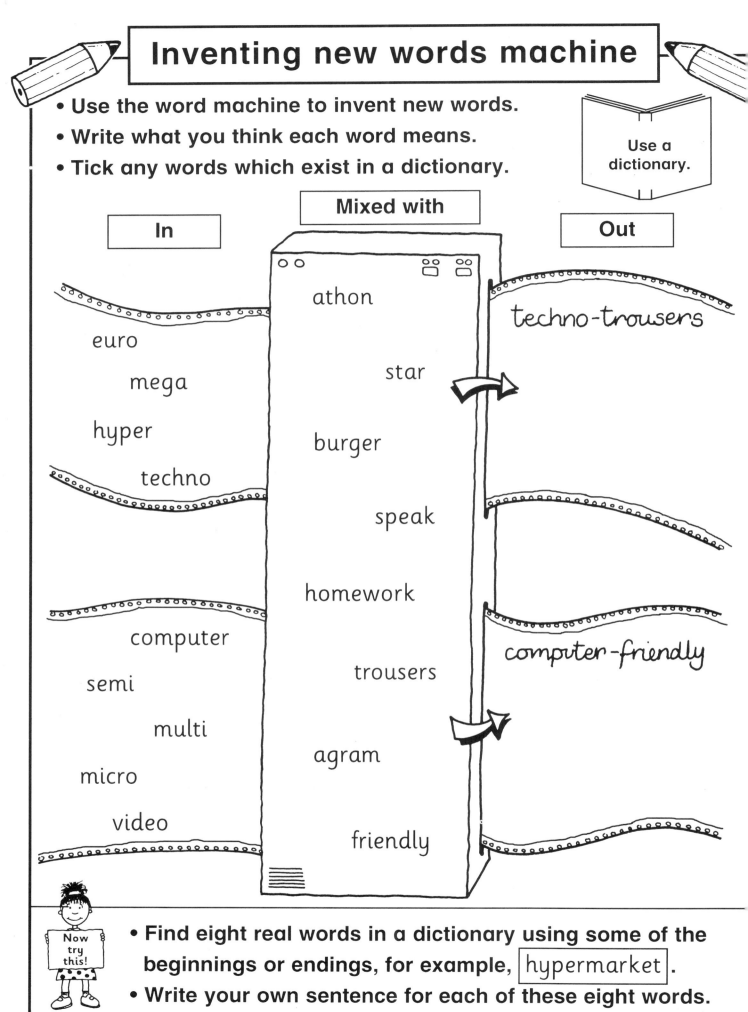

In

Mixed with

Out

euro

mega

hyper

techno

computer

semi

multi

micro

video

athon

star

burger

speak

homework

trousers

agram

friendly

techno-trousers

computer-friendly

Now try this!

- **Find eight real words in a dictionary using some of the beginnings or endings, for example,** hypermarket .
- **Write your own sentence for each of these eight words.**

Teachers' note The aim of this sheet is for the children to experiment with the structure of words and to build imaginary words using recognisable parts. Although the words will not exist in a dictionary, they can decide what the words might mean from the beginnings and endings.

Developing Literacy Year 4
© A & C Black 1998

Jigsaw words

- **Work with a partner. Cut out the root word cards.**
- **Take it in turns to fit two root word cards together to make real compound words.**
- **List all the compound words you have made.**

LSCWCh

Use a dictionary.

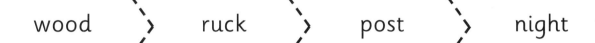

wood	ruck	post	night
wall	to	rain	key
farm	every	black	birth
mare	bow	day	worm
berry	board	box	yard
sack	morrow	one	paper

Teachers' note This can be played competitively or co-operatively. Another fun activity is to invent new compound words and then play a form of 'Call my bluff'. A child might suggest, for example, 'A rainboard is a wooden umbrella'.

Developing Literacy Year 4
© A & C Black 1998

Endings dice

- **Throw the die to find an ending. Choose a word from the notepad. Add the ending to make a real word.**
- **List the words you have made.**
- **Notice how some words change when you add a new ending, for example,** | type | + | ist | = | typist | .

support	reflect	attract	produce	slow
cube	science	comedy	cycle	geology
type	solo	cylinder	beauty	thought
sphere	thank	silent	patient	sudden

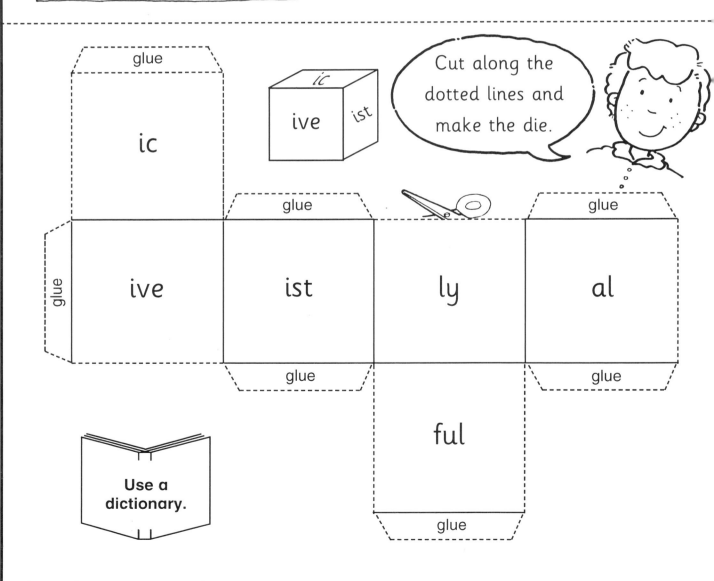

glue

ic

ive ist

Cut along the dotted lines and make the die.

glue   glue

glue

ive   ist   ly   al

glue   glue

ful

glue

Use a dictionary.

Teachers' note Photocopy or stick this page on to card. The children could work in pairs, co-operatively or competitively. One child throws the die and makes a new word while the other checks the word in the dictionary. Discuss the spelling changes that occur in some words.

Developing Literacy Year 4
© A & C Black 1998

Contents

KU-243-353

Supplementary units

Introduction

Scholastic Literacy Skills: Spelling is a structured spelling scheme for primary children from Years 3–6 (P4–7) and has been designed to meet children's spelling needs for these vital years of literacy development.

Good spelling is one of the most visible indications of literacy. It serves the purpose of good communication and marks the writer as one who has achieved a certain level of proficiency in literacy. It frees writers to concentrate more fully on the writing task itself. While it is important that children are given opportunities for 'free' writing, their ability to spell will not naturally improve if teaching only happens as and when individual needs arise.

Learning to spell is a developmental process and Scholastic Literacy Skills: Spelling focuses attention on the need for systematic teaching of spelling. An ongoing programme that involves the whole class in direct teaching is the best way to help children to become independent, effective spellers and fluent, confident writers. This is where Scholastic Literacy Skills: Spelling, with its unit-by-unit, context-based approach to learning and practising spellings, can help.

What should children know by the end of Year 2/P3?

Scholastic Literacy Skills: Spelling is developmentally structured to take children through the stages of spelling knowledge from Years 3–6 (P4–7). It is assumed that by the end of Year 2 (P3) children know all the letter names and sounds (especially the five vowels, and the use of the letter *y* as a vowel), both aurally and in written form. They should be able to form letters correctly and spell high-frequency words which observe common letter patterns (for example, *can, dog, man*). They should be able to spell some high-frequency but irregular words in terms of sight–sound correspondence (for example, *the, my, we*). The Dolch list of high-frequency words is given on page 23 and can be used (along with the National Literacy Strategy *Framework for Teaching* high- and medium-frequency words lists) as a quick assessment test of your class's spelling needs.

Spelling in the National Curriculum for England and Wales

Key Stage 1
Scholastic Literacy Skills: Spelling Ages 7–8 is aimed at the early stages of Key Stage 2, but it revises the following aspects of the National Curriculum for English. By the end of Key Stage 1, children should be able to:
- write each letter of the alphabet
- use their knowledge of sound–symbol relationships and phonological patterns
- recognise and use simple spelling patterns
- write common letter strings within familiar and common words
- spell commonly occurring simple words
- spell words with common prefixes and suffixes
- check the accuracy of their spelling, using wordbanks and dictionaries
- use their knowledge of word families and other words
- identify reasons for misspellings.

Key Stage 2

The National Curriculum for English at Key Stage 2 states that children should be taught:
● the meanings, uses and spellings of common prefixes and suffixes
● the spellings of words with inflectional endings
● the relevance of word families, roots and origins of words
● the use of appropriate terminology including *vowel, consonant, homophone* and *syllable*.

It also states that children should be taught the following spelling strategies:
● to sound out phonemes
● to analyse words into syllables and other known words
● to apply knowledge of spelling conventions
● to use knowledge of common letter strings, visual patterns and analogies
● to check their spelling using wordbanks, dictionaries and spellcheckers
● to revise and build on their knowledge of words and spelling patterns.

(from *The National Curriculum: Handbook for Primary Teachers in England* © Crown copyright 1999; © Qualifications and Curriculum Authority 1999)

Scholastic Literacy Skills: Spelling covers all the spelling strategies mentioned above. It introduces and explains rules, and provides opportunities for practice and revision. Using the Look–Say–Cover–Write–Check method of learning spellings, children learn to spell words and write them in personal wordbanks. They are encouraged to re-enter misspelled words into these wordbanks correctly. *Scholastic Literacy Skills: Spelling* introduces children to using a dictionary and gives practice in using a dictionary effectively (by direct teaching and regular practice). Children are also introduced to using an etymological dictionary and to using a thesaurus.

The 5–14 National Guidelines for Scotland

The 5–14 National Guidelines make specific reference to spelling in the English Language programmes of study: 'The teaching of spelling should be part of an agreed scheme… Supporting use should be made of a published spelling scheme graduated according to pupils' progress.' Explicit reference is made to the Look–Say–Cover–Write–Check strategy as being one method of teaching children to deal with mistakes. The 5–14 National Guidelines also make specific reference to the value of each child having a personal spelling book; this, in the form of the wordbank, is an important feature of *Scholastic Literacy Skills: Spelling*.

The Northern Ireland Curriculum

In discussing spelling within the context of the Writing Programme of Study, the Northern Ireland Curriculum outlines a broad progression at Key Stage 2 that reflects that built into *Scholastic Literacy Skills: Spelling* – 'from spelling common and familiar words in a recognisable way towards spelling more complex words correctly'. More specifically, it expects that at the end of Key Stage 2 children should be able to spell from memory frequently used words, to apply a variety of strategies to spell unfamiliar words and to use dictionaries and thesauruses. All these skills are addressed through *Scholastic Literacy Skills: Spelling*.

Common questions about spelling

Many teachers are unsure about how to teach spelling. Some common concerns are:
- How do I cope with varying levels of ability?
- How do I help children to look carefully at words so that they can recall them from memory and not just copy them 'thoughtlessly'?
- How do I help those children with specific difficulties in literacy-related areas?
- How do I encourage children to use dictionaries speedily and to locate the etymology of words?

Scholastic Literacy Skills: Spelling helps to answer these questions. It covers and continuously reviews all the areas of spelling required by the UK national curricula. Furthermore, it fulfils criteria for developing a holistic approach to literacy that links spelling, reading, writing, and speaking and listening.

A variety of strategies

Scholastic Literacy Skills: Spelling's approach to the teaching of spelling combines a variety of strategies based upon relevant research on how children learn to spell. These strategies include knowledge of:

1. Sound–symbol relationships

Much has been written about the irregularities in the English spelling system in terms of spelling according to the sounds we hear. In fact, the English writing system can be regarded as at least 80 per cent regular. Novice writers who spell according to sound (for example, *I haf a bic* for *I have a bike*) are able to communicate their message adequately, even if the spellings are incorrect.

It is, therefore, essential that children first learn the relationship between the names and the sounds of the 26 letters of the alphabet and also their appearance in graphic form. Later, children need to know the 44 sounds (or phonemes) in the English language (see page 22 for a list of the phonemes).

The research of Peter Bryant and Lynette Bradley, and Usha Goswami and Bryant, indicates that even very young children are usually sensitive to the sounds they hear. Children are particularly sensitive to rime (or what teachers may refer to approximately as rhyme) and onset (the first consonant/s in a word such as the *s* in *sing* and the *dr* in *drop*).

Findings indicate that children who are helped to develop their phonological awareness and sense of rhyme at an early age are likely to learn to read and spell more easily. A knowledge of the aural aspects of the writing process is integral to the approach in *Scholastic Literacy Skills: Spelling*.

2. Blends and digraphs

Though many children can detect and identify sounds in words, problems sometimes arise when they try to write what they hear as they say a word. Words which cause difficulty are those with letters that blend or run together when they are spoken (for example, *sing, stop*) or with two letters that have only one sound (these are called digraphs, of which *ea, ai, ch, ck, sh* are examples). *Scholastic Literacy Skills: Spelling* practises and revises common blends and digraphs, and encourages children to read texts aloud, listening for certain sounds while they look at the corresponding written form. This focus on careful listening and looking is a vital strategy in improving children's awareness of the 'trickier' aspects of the English spelling system.

3. Pronunciation of words

Teachers and parents can help children to spell by articulating words clearly and correctly and, when necessary, by drawing their attention to how a particular sound is voiced. It is even more helpful to show children how a particularly tricky sound looks in writing. Often, if children want to represent a sound when they are spelling a word, but have difficulty in finding a perfect fit, they will choose a near fit by using a letter that approximates to the sound they wish to represent. For example, children who have difficulty with the *th* digraph may say (and then write) *free* for *three*, or *tay/tey* for *they*. Similarly, it is common for some children to omit the *h* from *wh* words (for example, *whisper, when, where*). Some misspellings may be caused by difficulties in discriminating some sounds (see 'Helping children with spelling difficulties', page 18). Throughout *Scholastic Literacy Skills: Spelling*, children read texts aloud to themselves and/or others. Teachers may decide to read some texts aloud to the class, to model clear, correct pronunciation; this may differ according to regional accents so that, for example, the *u* sound in *book* may be pronounced as *oo*, especially in parts of Northern England.

4. Syllabification

The strategy of dividing words into syllables is helpful in several ways. It enables children to remember how to spell longer words by finding shorter, known words or roots within the longer word (for example, *know* and *edge* in *knowledge*). It can help them not to omit parts of longer words (for example, *en vi ron ment* or *dis app ear*) by focusing on short sound units (there are far fewer syllables than there are letters in the words). This strategy also reinforces correct pronunciation of words. Syllabification is a regular feature of activities in *Scholastic Literacy Skills: Spelling*.

5. Sight–symbol relationships

As novice spellers progress from the phonetic stage of spelling, they become increasingly aware that letter sounds do not always have a constant representation in writing. For example, the *as* in the word *was* is often written by novice spellers as *woz*. Such spellers begin to rely more on visual and morphemic (or meaning-bearing) clues, and need to pay special attention to the visual aspects of words. They need to work on developing a visual memory, locating difficult parts of words by looking carefully at tricky spellings. The ability to look carefully at words needs thoughtful and explicit teaching. In normal reading, it is possible to make sense of text while paying minimal attention to the spelling of individual words. A good visual memory is best achieved (especially for tricky words, for example those with irregular sound–symbol correspondences) by using the Look–Say–Cover–Write–Check method. Writers should then use the tricky words in the course of their own writing, or the words should form part of a contextualised writing activity.

6. Roots of words

Roots are the 'meaning-bearing chunks' of words. If learner spellers can identify roots, they can make sense of the fairly regular patterns of changes of meaning and spelling that occur when prefixes or suffixes are added to roots. They can then learn to build words and, conversely, to break them up to facilitate spelling, as explained in section 4 on the previous page.

7. Prefixes and suffixes from other languages

Prefixes and suffixes, when added to the root of a word, alter the meaning of the word. Many are of Latin or Greek origin. The earlier children are introduced to prefixes and suffixes, the better, as learning about them helps children to understand the meanings of new words, and consequently to spell them.

8. Word families

Independent, self-sufficient spelling should be the aim of every learner speller. A knowledge of word families (or word patterns) helps children to spell by analogy and to make an intelligent 'guess' at a spelling. It is important that children always 'have a go' at a spelling, so long as they then remember to check their guess. Word families are useful as a memory aid – the words can be put into a sentence to be learned, for example *I ought to have brought my books – I thought I had!* or *My friend has a piece of pie.* Encourage children to make up their own mnemonic sentences for words they find difficult. They could also collect new words for word families.

9. Kinaesthetic approaches

Kinaesthetic refers to the shape of a word. Kinaesthetic strategies, which involve using 3-D letters or letter shapes for children to move around to make words, or tracing over letters, are often recommended for children who experience difficulties with reading and spelling. In fact, many learner spellers benefit from this approach. The use of something tangible (for example, plastic letters or tracing in sand) can help make a learning task less abstract and transitory. For older learners, Scrabble tiles are an 'adult' version of the same approach.

10. Generalisations about the English spelling system

Many of the so-called 'rules' of spelling have exceptions to them. But if they are taught as generalisations with exceptions, they can provide a degree of security. *Scholastic Literacy Skills: Spelling* gives, practises and revises such rules in order to reduce the learning load.

Using *Scholastic Literacy Skills: Spelling*

Scholastic Literacy Skills: Spelling recognises that spelling is an integral part of the writing process, which includes grammar and punctuation, and requires an active approach so that children use and apply spellings in their reading and writing in all learning areas. It has been shown that learning spellings in isolation is not an effective way of ensuring this integration. *Scholastic Literacy Skills: Spelling* encourages children to work at improving their spelling in different contexts, giving relevance to the spelling task. It includes lively rhymes, poems, puzzles, jokes, short stories and information texts which hold children's attention, foster discussion and close engagement with texts. This approach gives real opportunities to both extend children's knowledge and to show them that learning to spell can be fun.

The four books in the series provide continuity, progression and flexibility for all the children in a class and are not merely collections of lists of words to be tested weekly. The supplementary photocopiable sheets in each book allow teachers to differentiate tasks even more finely, tailoring the units to suit individual needs.

General approaches

Scholastic Literacy Skills: Spelling is designed to be used flexibly in the classroom. Teachers will decide which approaches best suit their children. Some general approaches are:

Whole-class approach

If each child has a copy of the same unit, the spelling needs of the children can be met through progress as a class. This allows the whole class to work simultaneously on a shared text.

Group approach

This approach enables different-ability groups to work on different units. *Scholastic Literacy Skills: Spelling* caters for sequential development so that each photocopiable book dovetails into the next. This provides opportunities for flexible planning of a spelling programme. Exercises can be related to ongoing class work and/or projects. So, for example, when adjectives and nouns are discussed, it might be helpful to look at *Spelling Ages 8–9* (pages 70–1); or if word origins are discussed, the units on etymology in *Spelling Ages 9–10* (pages 64–5 and 92–3) could be used.

Skills-focus approach

Scholastic Literacy Skills: Spelling permits a systematic development of spelling skills suited to the different linguistic levels of children. In a class of eight- to nine-year-olds, for example, children of average ability in spelling (which may be most of the class) may work on units from *Spelling Ages 8–9*, while more able spellers work on units from *Spelling Ages 9–10*. Children who find spelling difficult may work on units from *Spelling Ages 7–8*, using the supplementary photocopiable pages to reinforce learning.

Teachers could spend between five and ten minutes explaining work to the 'average' spellers, while the less able spellers could be paired to test each other on spellings entered in their wordbanks. More able spellers could begin working unaided (initially). This helps children become accustomed to following instructions independently. After the first five or ten minutes, teachers will be available to give time to the less able spellers, explaining tasks carefully, checking their self-tests or revising recently learned work.

Using the units

Teachers can read instructions, poems and texts both to and with the children, especially less able spellers and readers. This is particularly recommended when using units from the books for *Spelling Ages 7–8* and *Spelling Ages 8–9*.

Make sure that children become familiar with the technical vocabulary used in the units (for example, *underline, complete, fill in, consonant, vowel (long* and *short), singular, plural* and so on). Don't forget that some children have difficulties in distinguishing left from right.

Ensure that children understand fully the Look–Say–Cover–Write–Check method of learning spellings. Encourage them to look carefully and to identify and underline tricky words or parts of words. Many novice spellers simply glance at a word to be learned without noting the shape of the individual letters. Model this strategy explicitly and often. Remind children regularly of the strategy when undertaking written work.

Effective proof-reading also requires modelling. The checking of work needs to be done quite slowly, word by word, if errors are to be detected. Making up mnemonics is something children enjoy, but remind them that their purpose is to remember how to spell a word. For example, if the sentence *The bus is busy* is used to aid the spelling of *bus*, then it should be explained that *busy* contains the word *bus*; this part of the word should be underlined.

Wordbanks

A photocopiable wordbank is provided on pages 112–8. It lists every word taught in the main units of this book, and has alphabetical headings so that children can have practice in developing skills using alphabetical order.

Setting up children's individual wordbanks is also important and children should be encouraged to use theirs as a quick reference for all written work. This should become a matter of instinct for children, but in the early stages regular use needs to be encouraged. Some children may be reluctant to re-enter words they misspell. It is, however, vital that they do re-enter words (particularly high-frequency words) that cause them difficulty. Each child and teacher will then be able to flick through the wordbank and quickly identify tricky words. For example, if *because* is entered three or four times, this indicates that the word needs specific attention.

Targeting tricky words

In the course of working on the activities, children are asked to make up their own sentences using target words. Encourage children to use words they have learned but found tricky. This means they will constantly revise high-frequency words that they find difficult. For example, if two of the words appearing several times in a child's wordbank are *because* and *should*, and an exercise asks for original sentences using words ending in *tion*, the child may write: *He **should** go to the sta**tion because** his friend is coming by train.*

Review units

The review units, which occur after every six units in the main section of the book, provide records of individual progress and highlight difficulties. Pairs of children can use the pages to test each other. Discuss progress with individual children, noting any difficulties that need specific attention.

Make sure children understand each part of the Look–Say–Cover–Write–Check method of learning spellings. It is important that they look carefully at the words to improve their visual memory. Saying the words helps them to associate the sounds with the visual appearance of the letters. Writing the words helps them to 'feel' the shape of the letters through the hand, especially if joined-up handwriting is encouraged from an early age. They must understand how and why to check their written work, using their wordbank or a dictionary to confirm that either their spellings are correct or that further practice may be needed.

Involving parents

Parents can give vital help, support and encouragement to their children as they progress towards becoming effective spellers. If parents are to support their children positively so that spellings are regarded as part of the wider writing process and not simply a list of unconnected words, they need to be made aware of the school's approach to teaching and improving spelling. Invite parents who are willing to help their children with their written work into school and talk through the school's philosophy and strategies for teaching writing and spelling.

Encourage parents to:
- take an interest in their child's writing at home. They should read it and give relevant praise for effort and content. They should avoid commenting firstly (or worse still only) on spelling errors, presentation and handwriting.
- involve their child in 'real' writing tasks, such as shopping lists, invitations, letters and notes to friends and relatives, diary entries and similar activities.
- help their child to 'edit' their written work and encourage the use of wordbanks and/or dictionaries to check spellings.
- have spelling games for fun – in the car, around the table, at bedtime.
- use the Look–Say–Cover–Write–Check approach to learning to spell words. Parents may need careful, explicit demonstrations of this method if they did not encounter it in their school days.
- hear their child spell for fun.
- help their child to be aware of spellings around them, for example instructions on videos or washing machines; road signs; food labels. This awareness does not mean that the child has to learn the spellings, but it helps to impress the importance of written communication as part of everyday life.

Above all, stress to parents that learning sessions should be brief and fun, and should always include plenty of praise for effort and progress. Involving parents in this way helps to develop a positive attitude in the child, which is such an important part of becoming an effective and independent speller.

How to correct spellings

Encouraging children to identify problem words and tricky parts of words for themselves begins the process of developing a 'spelling conscience', which is an important part of being an effective speller. At all times, encourage children to look up and check words they are unsure of, or words which do not 'look right'. There will be occasions when you need to correct children's spelling in the course of written work. Some useful tips for correcting children's work sensitively are:
- Concentrate on correcting misspellings of words that the child ought to know how to spell at this stage (as class teacher you are in the best position to judge what these are). This not only guarantees the best use of (your) marking time but is also less demotivating for the child.
- Don't let misspellings get in the way of praise for overall writing content.
- Try to distinguish between misspelled words that should be familiar to the child, and those which are guesses at spelling new words. Judge the latter as guesses and praise good attempts – for example, the number of 'correct' letters or a good

approximation to the sound of the word or evident use of analogy (even if it is wrong).
● Whenever possible, write the whole word correctly for the child in the margin. Do not correct parts of words in the child's writing – this only confuses the writer.

Testing and assessment

Persistent misspellings are often a problem and it is important to give specific attention to children who are not progressing. Individual error analysis, not unlike the miscue analysis developed for reading, enables teachers to look more closely at the types of errors a child is making. Repeated misspellings of particular consonants, problems with spelling prefixes or vowel digraphs can be given special attention. Although time-consuming, such analysis gives important and useful information about particular areas of spelling weakness, which can then be targeted.

A simple grid can be developed to do this:

Individual error analysis sheet

Correct word	Attempted spelling	Type of error					
		initial consonant	final consonant	consonant blend	vowel	digraph	omission
cat	kat	✕					
bed	bet		✕				
stop	slop			✕			
run	ran				✕		
feet	fet					✕	
ship	sip					✕	

A photocopiable version of this grid can be found on page 27.

Screening tests

When Sybil Hannovy worked at the Cambridge Institute of Education, she constructed some tests that could be given to up to 20 children at a time by one teacher with another teacher in attendance. The tests take 45–60 minutes to administer. Though designed for children younger than seven years old, the writing parts of Hannovy's tests can be adapted for use with older children who are experiencing spelling difficulties.

We expect seven-year-olds to be able to hear and discriminate all the letter sounds and names as well as to be able to write them, but this is not always the case. Older children may also have difficulty with sound–symbol relationships, and knowledge of sound–symbol correspondence is a vital element in learning both to read and spell.

The following four tests are adaptations of some of Hannovy's tests that apply to the written aspects of literacy. Extend or amend the tests further to suit the needs of particular children in your class. The first three tests highlight the child's ability to connect phonemes with letters (the auditory aspects of spelling).

In the early stages of literacy acquisition, it is essential that children are able to make connections between what they hear and what they write. Once they can hear sounds correctly and can transfer what they hear into written forms, then they are ready to progress to the visual and memory stage. Research indicates that the number of letters children can identify before they start school is the strongest predictor of subsequent reading ability.

There should be no writing or alphabets visible while the children are taking the tests. You may wish to put folded screens of card between the children to prevent copying. However, this is unnecessary if only a few children are being tested.

1. Letter sounds

Say a word to the children, and repeat the initial sound. The children write the initial letter. Walk round to observe how each child is holding their pen or pencil; look at their writing posture and letter formation. Children who cannot write the answer may leave a space. Make sure that all the letters of the alphabet are tested, but not in alphabetical order. The letters *x*, *q* and *y* could be merely said aloud, using their letter names. Include words with common initial digraphs and blends, repeating the initial digraph or blend (for example, *ship, this, chip, Philip, clock, quick, slid, bright*). The complexity of vocabulary digraphs or blends you choose will depend on the written work of your class.

Using the results

This test highlights those letters with which children are having difficulty. Many letter sounds are similar in the way they are made. For example, the letter sounds *b*, *g* and *d* sound similar. In linguistics, these sounds are called stops since they 'stop' the air. Other sounds that are similar are the fricatives (made by the friction or restriction of breath in a narrow opening) such as *s, z, v, f* and *th* (as in *then* and *thin*, which some children hear and pronounce as *ven* or *fin*). The short vowel sounds (as in *pat, pet, pit, pot, put*) are also formed in similar ways (the tongue is held in slightly different positions as voiced air passes through the mouth) and can cause problems for novice writers of any age. Children who have taken the test and confused letters or left spaces may:
● be unable to differentiate aurally between certain letters, or
● lack knowledge of the correspondence between sounds and the formation of their written representation.

Having identified children's specific difficulties, you are in a position to target teaching on problem letters. Help children to identify their problem letters singly and within words aurally, before transferring them to their written form. Once single-letter difficulties have been remedied, move on to blends and digraphs that are difficult for the children. Demonstrate how 'difficult' sounds, blends and digraphs are made by exaggerating their oral formation.

2. Written vocabulary

Ask the children to write all the words they can remember in five (or more) minutes. It is essential that, at the end of the test, they read all their words aloud to the teacher to check their ability to read aloud their own writing. Some children might write *came*, for example, but then say *come*.

Using the results

This test indicates the general extent of words that the child can recall and write 'easily'. Use these 'known' words to construct further dictation exercises to improve and remedy spelling difficulties. Since these words will generally be those that the child can write confidently, they should make a good balance between new and past successful learning.

The test also reveals whether a child confuses formation of certain letters. For example, having written *wat* or **bog**, the child may say *wet* and **dog** when reading the words aloud after the test. The first error indicates confusion about the pronunciation of short vowel sounds. The second error indicates the confusion of *b* and *d*, which is a common characteristic of novice readers and writers.

To remedy the first error, spend time with the child, identifying confused vowel sounds both in isolation and within words. To tackle the second, ensure that the child is in fact able to differentiate between the sounds in spoken words. Then suggest that the child says *bat and ball* to him- or herself when forming the letter *b* (as the downstroke is formed, the child says *bat*, and as the circular movement is made, the child says *ball*). Similarly, when the child hears the *d* sound in a word, he or she should say *drum and stick* to him- or herself (as the circular part is formed, he or she says *drum* and he or she says *stick* as the downstroke is formed).

3. Three phonemes

Dictate approximately 20 three-letter words to the children for them to write down (Hannovy suggested ten words for Year 1 children). The words should include as many different consonants as possible and all the vowels (for example, *rap, beg, cot, dim, fun, hop, jig, keg, lap, sat, van, win, fox, yes, zip*). The four-letter words *quit* and *very* could be included to check the *q* sound and *y* as a vowel sound. Words containing letters and sounds that seem to be causing difficulties for particular children should also be included.

Using the results

This test reveals the child's ability to hear and differentiate consonants at the beginning and end of words, and vowel sounds within words. It reveals the child's ability to spell phonically regular words – that is, their ability to blend phonemes as well as to identify them within a given word. This test can reveal whether children can hear first and last letters clearly but not the middle vowel. For example, they might write *pn* for *pin*. Use the results of the test to work with children on specific difficulties, using letters both in isolation and in three- or four-letter words spoken and written by the child. Subsequently, incorporate the words into brief sentences for the child to write and say regularly until he or she can write them fluently. Such sentences will be very obviously contrived, but in the early stages of remediation, a child's success in the learning task is of paramount importance. Success leads to increased self-confidence and motivates the child to learn more. Keep such targeted teaching sessions brief, regular and explicit, and praise effort as well as success.

4. Sentence dictation

Dictate between four and six sentences, reading each one several times, slowly. The sentences should contain words that are familiar to the children, both aurally and visually. They should include regular and irregular spellings in terms of sound–letter correspondence. The Dolch list of high-frequency words (see page 23) is a good source of such words, as are the high- and medium-frequency lists in the National Literacy Strategy *Framework for Teaching*.

Using the results

This test gives information on the general spelling strategies used by the child. These examples are taken from three children's answers to a dictation test. The dictation sentences were:

> *He went in the house and saw a man.*
> *The man was doing some magic tricks.*

Child A wrote:
He went in the huose and saw a man.
The man was doing some magick tricks.

Child A shows only two errors. The first error, *huose*, contains all the correct letters, indicating visual recall of the word, but with confused recall of the *ou* sequence. The second error, *magick*, may be influenced by the spelling of the next word, *trick*. Once the child has identified and underlined the errors, look at other words in the *ou* family (for example, **out, our, loud, mouse**), and discuss the use of *c* and *ck* as word endings. Construct a sentence for the child to learn and be tested on over the following few days (for example, *I went **out** of **our** **house** with the magi**c** man*). If reversals of *ou* persist, compose a mnemonic for the *ou* sequence (for example, **Oh you** are in my h**ou**se).

Child B wrote:
He wet in the hows and saw a man.
The man woss dowing sum majik trix.

Child B shows that most (if not all) letter sounds are known, as many of the words are written according to their sound. Child B is still at what may be termed the 'invented' spelling stage. This child has minimal knowledge of high-frequency words with irregular sound–letter correspondence (for example, *he, saw, the*).

Show Child B explicitly how to look at problem words carefully and to identify the tricky parts for him- or herself. Use the child's errors to do this. For example, when looking at the word *doing* (which the child spelled *dowing*), praise him or her for having nearly all the correct letters, before asking him or her to spot the incorrect letter. Ask the child to use Look–Say–Cover–Write–Check to learn the words *do, doing, go, going*. To remedy *woss* for *was*, encourage the child to locate the word *as* within *was*.

Construct a sentence for the child to learn and be tested on over the following few days (for example, *He **was** not **do**ing his jobs, he was **go**ing in the hut*). Note that the 'new' words in the sentence are phonically regular and so should not cause difficulties for the child.

Adjust the learning load to suit different children's levels of difficulty and attention span.

> **Child C** wrote:
> *He we in the os a se a ma.*
> *The ma wos dwig mha tx.*

Child C's attempts at written communication have broken down completely. This child knows how to spell *he*, *in* and *the*, but leaves many words unfinished. Initial letters of words are generally correct; *os* for *house* indicates that the *h* has not been heard, or that the child is hearing the *o* and *s* sound more dominantly. This child's spelling strategies are characteristic of someone at the very earliest stage of learning to write and who has learned a few high-frequency words by heart. Identifying separate letters in words and blending letters will help this child.

Helping children with spelling difficulties

Regular reading and writing activities will help most children to become confident and efficient spellers. However, some children will find that learning to spell presents difficulties, and there are specific but varying causes for this. One cause is dyslexia whereby something goes wrong with a person's perception of words and letters. This often affects the ability to read and write. However, if teaching is tailored to individual needs, specific difficulties may be overcome. It is important, therefore, to try to find out the individual causes of these difficulties before attempts are made to remedy them.

Remediation may include teaching/revising one or more of the following:
- sound–symbol correspondence of the alphabet, including names of letters
- common and regular letter strings which may include the use of plastic letters
- awareness of irregular but high-frequency words in which the visual aspects of the words are studied
- clear articulation of words to be studied and clear articulation of the letters of the words (in sequence)
- multi-sensory approaches to the Look–Say–Cover–Write–Check method
- use of computers, word-processors, coloured pens and so on to aid motivation in learning
- use of mnemonics to aid learning
- regular use of wordbanks once spelling is improving
- very brief, but regular, informal tests on one or two sentences which contain the words learned – the aim is to ensure the child's success.

Using plastic letters to improve literacy

A useful tool for helping children with spelling difficulties is the use of plastic letters in instruction. Some research shows that less able readers (and spellers) may be unsuccessful in the aural medium since it seems too abstract. Working with the concrete and tangible, such as plastic letters, can help these children. When word building with plastic letters, keep the focus letters static while moving other letters around them. (For example, the blend *an* is kept static while *c, m, p, h* and *d, s* and *d* are placed in front and behind to make the words *an, can, man, pan, hand, sand*). Increase the complexity and difficulty of letter strings as the child progresses.

Look–Say–Cover–Write–Check

Expand the method into the following multi-sensory approach for children with difficulties. Children should:

1. **Look** carefully at the word.
2. **Say** the word and then its letters (names) in sequence.
3. **Cover** the word up.
4. **'Write'** the word, saying the whole word first, then the letter names:
   - in the air with eyes closed, or
   - on an (imaginary) desk, or
   - in wet sand.
   If all appears to be correct, then say the word and its letters to the teacher. Write the word on paper or in a wordbank (saying the word and letter names while doing so).
5. **Check** the word. If it is correct, write a tick over each correct letter, adding an extra tick if all the letters are in the correct order*.

*This way, the child feels more involved in his or her learning and progress than if the teacher takes the child's work and applies ticks (or crosses). For example, *house* would receive six ticks (one for each correct letter, and one for the correct sequence); *huose* would receive five ticks; and *hows* four ticks (one for each correct letter and one because they are in the correct order).

These procedures may seem time-consuming, but they usually apply only to a few children with severe spelling difficulties.

Motivating children with spelling difficulties

Using ICT can help to motivate children who find spelling difficult, particularly older children who are more likely to be negative in their attitude towards remedial teaching than younger ones. Word-processing, for example, can be helpful in giving higher status to the writing process – the work produced is clear and professional, and inputting words on-screen reinforces understanding of the left-to-right sequence of writing. Increasingly, even very young children are able to find their way round technological equipment, sometimes more easily than adults.

Encourage children to use computer spellcheckers. They will not impede the process of learning to spell and can be a useful aid, if children know about the pitfalls of using them. Make sure they understand that spellcheckers do not eliminate errors entirely as they cannot recognise grammatical relationships in sentences. It is important that children know when to 'overrule' the spellchecker.

Once confidence in spelling has been restored, and progress made and maintained, children should balance traditional methods of writing with using the computer. The use of coloured pens, pencils and paper can also stimulate children's motivation.

Bibliography

Bryant, PE & Bradley, L (1985) *Rhyme and Reason in Reading and Spelling*, University of Michigan Press.

DfEE/QCA (1999) *The National Curriculum: Handbook for Primary Teachers in England*.

Department of Education Northern Ireland (1996) *The Northern Ireland Curriculum Key Stages 1 and 2*.

Ehri, LC (1991) 'Learning to read and spell words' in L Rieben and C Perfetti (eds) *Learning to Read: Basic Research and its Implications*, Lawrence Erlbaum Associates.

Goswami, U & Bryant, PE (1990) *Phonological Skills and Learning to Read*, Lawrence Erlbaum Associates.

Hannovy, S (1991) 'Middle infant screening test: a safety net for teachers' in *Reading*, 25, no. 3, 10–15, Blackwell for UKRA.

Morris, JM (1984) 'Phonics 44 for initial literacy in English' in *Reading*, 18, no. 1, Blackwell for UKRA.

Mudd, NR (1994) *Effective Spelling: A practical guide for teachers*, Hodder & Stoughton in association with UKRA.

Peters, ML (1985) *Spelling: Caught or Taught? (A New Look)*, Routledge.

The Scottish Office Education Department (1991) *National Guidelines English Language 5–14*.

Temple, C, Nathan, R, Burris, N & Temple, F (1993 3rd edition) *The Beginnings of Writing*, Allyn and Bacon Inc.

Todd, J (1982) *Learning to Spell: A Book of Resources for Teachers*, Simon & Schuster.

Teaching content and skills grid

- Reinforces children's knowledge of English words derived from Latin and Greek words, especially the use of prefixes to improve and extend vocabulary as well as spelling. Vocabulary development is accompanied by sentences illustrating the meaning of new words.
- Enables children to use dictionaries effectively – that is, accurately and speedily, in order to check spellings and to discover or check word meanings.
- Introduces the use of a thesaurus. Children have opportunities to find suitable words to express meanings and are urged to avoid overusing words such as *nice, go, a lot of*.
- Encourages the use of etymological dictionaries to locate word origins, such as that of *igloo*.
- Revises high-frequency words (especially homophones) that may be causing difficulties. Children continue to identify 'tricky' parts of words by underlining them.
- Revises words covered and revisits spelling rules. The correct use of grammatical vocabulary is made.
- Continues the Look–Say–Cover–Write–Check method of learning spellings.
The grid on the facing page matches teaching content to pages.

List of the 44 phonemes in English

20 vowel sounds

Short vowel sounds

apple
egg
ink
orange
umbrella
potato (this has an indistinct vowel sound or *schwa*)

Long vowel sounds

ape	pain	say
eve	peel	seal
ice	lie	high
mode	soak	toe
flute	pool	

Other vowel sounds

ball	walk	saw
star		
bird	hermit	
hook		
mouth	clown	
coil	boy	
square	chair	
ear	deer	here
gourd	poor	

24 consonant sounds

bat
cat (kit)
din
fish
go
have
jump
let
man
net
pat
run
set
tap
violin
want
yet
zoo (houses)
shop
chin
the
thing
sing
television

Some other consonant patterns

double consonants: *ff, ck*
clusters (initial): *sk, sp, st, cl, cr, scr, str*
clusters (end): *sk, sp, st, ps, nds, nks*
silent letters: *knit, thumb*

NB *q* and *x* are redundant as 'basic' phonemes.

Dolch list

These 100 words make up, on average, one half of all reading.

a	and	he
I	in	is
it	of	that
the	to	was
all	as	at
be	but	are
for	had	have
his	him	not
on	one	said
so	they	we
with	you	about
an	back	been
before	big	by
call	came	can
come	could	did
do	down	first
from	get	go
has	her	here
if	into	just
like	little	look
made	make	more
me	much	must
my	no	new
now	off	old
only	or	our
other	out	over
right	see	she
some	their	them
then	there	this
two	up	want
well	went	were
what	when	where
which	will	who
your		

The 100 next most used words.

after	again	always
am	another	any
away	ask	bad
because	best	bird
black	blue	boy
bring	day	dog
don't	eat	every
far	fast	father
fell	find	five
fly	four	found
gave	girl	give
going	good	got
green	hand	have
head	help	home
house	how	jump
keep	know	last
left	let	live
long	man	many
may	men	mother
Mr	never	next
once	open	own
play	put	ran
read	red	room
round	run	sat
saw	say	school
should	sing	sit
soon	stop	take
tell	than	these
thing	think	three
time	too	tree
under	us	very
walk	white	why
wish	work	would
year		

Name _____   Date _____

Am I a good speller?

	often	sometimes	never
I know that correct spelling is important.			
I always stop to check a spelling if I am unsure			
• by checking in my wordbank			
• by checking in a dictionary.			
I always proof-read by looking for spelling mistakes.			
I take care with my handwriting.			
I notice letter patterns like **th** and **ough**.			
I notice suffixes like **-less**.			
I notice prefixes like **dis-**.			
I learn new spellings using Look–Say–Cover–Write–Check.			
I make up mnemonics to help me remember spellings.			
My tricky words are			

Scholastic Literacy Skills
Spelling Ages 10–11

Photocopiable ◪ SCHOLASTIC

Name _____   Date _____

Indicators for novice spellers

Spelling confidence:	often	sometimes	never
spells known words automatically			
interested in new words			
tackles spellings of new words with intelligent guesses			
Spelling conscience:			
proof-reads own writing			
checks words unsure of			
● using the wordbank			
● using a dictionary			
Spelling skills:			
aware of visual patterns			
recognises many common words			
is able to spell many common words			
uses words with irregular spellings			
attempts to spell new words by analogy			
uses syllabification to learn longer words			
uses mnemonics			
understands compound words			
uses common prefixes and suffixes			
recognises roots of words			
aware that there are different ways of spelling a sound			

Record of progress

Units	
1 Going to the circus	
2 Local attack	
3 Sports time	
4 The highwayman	
5 On the train	
6 It's mine	
7 Hovercrafts and headaches	
8 I'm amazed!	
9 Take care	
10 Practice makes perfect	
11 Be prepared	
12 Say it correctly!	
13 To the mountains	
14 A stupid thing to do	
15 Excursions and discussions	
16 Admirable adjectives	
17 Stop and think	
18 Stanfield Bay	
19 Flight to Perth	
20 In the quagmire	
21 Be silent!	
22 It's tricky	
23 Lessen the load	
24 Find it quickly	
25 A trip overseas	
26 Let's stay together	
27 Remember the 'h'	
28 Oh crumbs!	
29 Don't leave it out	
30 Many things	
31 Thirsty work	
32 Explorers	
33 Drop it or double it	
34 Be innovative	
35 Where does it come from?	
36 Edit and proof-read	

Name   Date

Individual error analysis sheet

Correct word	Attempted spelling	Type of error					
		initial consonant	final consonant	consonant blend	vowel	digraph	omission

Name

Going to the circus

1. Read this passage aloud. Underline all the **o** sounds.

The circus had taken over the showground. Joe Burrows watched the men slowly erect the tent. He listened to their moans and groans as they pulled the tent up the centre pole.

He wanted to go to the circus, so he walked over to a man who was throwing gear onto a truck. "What do you want, kid?" he asked in a croaky voice.

"I want to go to the circus, but I don't have any cash," said Joe.

"No dosh, eh? Want to earn some?"

"OK," he said, not wanting to feel a goat.

Joe worked at the circus all day and went home cold and tired. His mum thought that he had been playing with his friends. She didn't know that he had been working to earn money! She was very cross with him.

"I could have paid for us to go," she said. "There was no need to do that, Joe."

"I'm sorry," said Joe. "I thought I was being grown-up. We can still go, can't we, Mum?"

"Oh, all right then," said Mrs Burrows.

They arrived at the showground and Joe's mum went up to the ticket window. There was a notice on the window: 'Sold Out'.

But they saw the show because the man with the croaky voice had left tickets there for them.

 The **o** sound, as in **go, hole, toe, cold, boat, blow, soul**, is spelled in many different ways. Watch out for the different spellings!

2. Write any new **o** sound words in your wordbank.

3. Add one or two more words to each of these word families.

go	o-	toe	dole	cold	boat	blow	mould
so	open	roe	hole	bold	coat	flow	boulder

Photocopiable **SCHOLASTIC** Continued on

Name

Objective: Spell words in which the final consonant is doubled when adding *ing* or *ed.*

nued from P28

 **Unit 1**

> When we add a suffix to words which end in consonant–vowel–consonant (CVC), we double the final consonant.
>
> For example: run (CVC) + ing = ru**nn**ing

5. Look at these words. Say them aloud.

bed	–	bedding	spot	– spotting	nod	–	nodded
bat	–	batting	fit	– fitted	plan	–	planned
clip	–	clipping	mat	– matted	slam	–	slammed
bet	–	betting					

6. Add **ing** to these words. Write the new words below.

flap _____   tug _____   ship _____

step _____   stop _____   rob _____

wrap _____   plug _____   swim _____

7. Add **ed** to these words. Write the new words below.

beg _____   top _____   spot _____

chop _____   tip _____   rot _____

pin _____   strip _____   hop _____

wag _____

8. In these words of more than one syllable, the CVC 'rule' still works. Add **ing** to these words. Write the new words below.

occur _____   tunnel _____

prefer _____   forget _____

travel _____   model _____

control _____

9. Use Look–Say–Cover–Write–Check to enter any new words in your wordbank.

Photocopiable ■ **SCHOLASTIC**

Name

Local attack

 Usually, when we add a suffix to a word which ends in a consonant–vowel–consonant (CVC), we double the final consonant.

1. Add **ed** to these words. Write the new words below.

trip   cancel   quarrel   ship   transfer

_____   _____   _____   _____   _____

2. Add suffixes **er, ing, ed** to these words.

	er	**ing**	**ed**
spot	_Spotter_	_spotting_	_spotted_
kidnap	_____	_____	_____
travel	_____	_____	_____
plan	_____	_____	_____

 A word which doesn't follow the rule is:

orbit   orbiter   orbiting   orbited

3. Read this passage. Fill in the spaces, choosing from the root words in the box and adding the correct suffix.

travel   kidnap   rob   plan   worship   quarrel

Local attack

A young tr_____ was ki_____ and ro_____ while visiting a local

church graveyard. The thieves had pl_____ the attack well as there were no

wo_____ in the churchyard at the time. They pushed the young tr_____

into the back seat of their car. The ki_____ seemed to be qu_____ with

each other at the time of the attack.

Photocopiable ■ SCHOLASTIC Continued on

Name

inued from P30　　　　　　　　　　　　　　　　　　　　　　

Some words ending in CVC do *not* double the final consonant when a suffix is added.

4. Say these words aloud.　(suffer　suffering　suffered　sufferer)

5. Read these words aloud, then add **ed** or **ing** to each. Write the new words below.

ing　　　　　　　　　　　　　　　　**ed**

blossom _____　　open _____

benefit _____　　visit _____

flower _____　　plaster _____

powder _____　　suffer _____

6. Read these words aloud, adding **ed** or **ing** to each. Write the new words below. **Be careful!** Some of these words are not CVC words.

ed　　　　　　　　　　　　　　　　**ing**

add _____　　hatch _____

afford _____　　jump _____

tap _____　　knock _____

count _____　　lend _____

refer _____　　prop _____

drop _____　　paint _____

crowd _____　　pass _____

curl _____　　propel _____

stir _____　　search _____

hand _____　　sigh _____

Name

Objective: Investigate the present tense and present participle, past tense and past participle.

Unit 3

Sports time

Verbs change their spelling depending on how they are used.
For example: To be fit you have **to train**.

present tense	you **train**
past tense	you **trained**
present tense and participle	you are **training**
past tense and participle	you have **trained**

The changes in the verb **to train** are quite easy. You just add **ing** or **ed**. Some verbs are more difficult. For example: **to swim**

present tense	you **swim**
past tense	you **swam**
present tense and participle	you are **swimming**
past tense and participle	you have **swum**

Fill in the missing parts of the verbs. Some have been done for you.

verb	present participle	past tense	past participle
swim	swimming	swam	swum
jump		jumped	
	throwing		
climb			
catch			
drive			
ride			

2. Read this story, using the correct forms of the verbs in brackets to fill the spaces.

I like (climb)_____ because it is a daring sport. I have

(hear) _____ that people have had serious injuries because

they have (fall) _____ from the rocks. To climb safely you

must be well (train) _____ and properly equipped.

Name

inued from P32   Unit 3

> Adjectives change their spelling depending on how they are used.
> For example: I am happ**y**   you are happ**ier**   he is happ**iest**
>
> Like verbs, adjectives can be difficult when you alter their meaning.
> For example: I am **bad**   you are **worse**   he is **worst**

3. Fill in the missing words in each column.
The first one has been done for you.

fit   *fitter*   *fittest*

fast   _____   _____

good   _____   _____

healthy _____   _____

strong   _____   _____

The adjectives in the second and third columns are called adjectives of comparison. Can you think why?

> Some adjectives do not take **er** and **est**. You have to add **more** or **most** to them like this:
>   different   more different   most different

4. Fill in the missing words in each column. The first one has been done for you.

beautiful   *more beautiful*   *most beautiful*

skilful   _____   _____

dangerous   _____   _____

5. Read this passage. Complete the last two sentences with the correct adjectives of comparison.

My brother, the weightlifter

My first brother is big, strong, mighty, muscular and powerful.

My second brother is bigger, _____, _____, more

_____ and more _____.

My third brother is the biggest, _____, _____, most

_____ and most _____ – and he writes poetry.

Photocopiable ■ SCHOLASTIC

The highwayman

1. Read these two verses. They have been taken from a poem called 'The highwayman'. They describe how a highwayman travelled to an inn to meet his sweetheart, Bess.

The highwayman

The wind was a torrent of darkness among the gusty trees,

The moon was a ghostly galleon tossed upon cloudy seas,

The road was a ribbon of moonlight over the purple moor,

And the highwayman came riding

Riding – riding –

The highwayman came riding, up to the old inn-door.

Over the cobbles he clattered and clashed in the dark inn-yard.

He tapped with his whip on the shutters, but all was locked and barred.

He whistled a tune to the window, and who should be waiting there

But the landlord's black-eyed daughter,

Bess, the landlord's daughter,

Plaiting a dark red love-knot into her long black hair.

Alfred Noyes

2. Underline all the words which have a **silent h** or a **silent k**.

3. Write any new words in your wordbank.

Objective: Spell words with silent letters *h* and *k*.

4. Read these **silent h** and **silent k** words aloud.

g**h**ostly	g**h**astly	g**h**erkin	g**h**etto

honour
honest } (Don't sound the **h**!)

knot	**k**night	**k**nee	**k**napsack
khaki	**k**nave	**k**nell	**k**nuckle

5. Look up the meanings of any words new to you and write them, with their meanings, in your wordbank. Use Look–Say–Cover–Write–Check.

6. Read these sentences, then fill in the spaces with some of the **silent h** and **silent k** words.

The traveller's k_____ was made of canvas.

The party was held in h_____ of her 21st birthday.

Did you hurt your k_____s when you hit the wall with your fist?

Our uniform was a dull k_____ colour.

My grandmother called dishonest men k_____s.

A g_____ is a type of small cucumber used in jars of pickles.

The moon was a g_____ galleon tossed upon cloudy seas.

She plaited a dark red love-k_____ into her long black hair.

7. Now write the completed sentences in your workbook. Try to write the missing words from *memory*.

On the train

1. Read this beginning of a story.

Unfinished story

It was cold in the train.

"I want to go to the toilet."

"Hold on," said Mum.

I held on, but it got worse.

"Mum, I need to go to the toilet."

"I told you that you would have to hold on. I can't do anything

about it. You should have gone before we left home."

I tried to think of other things. I watched a fly crawl on the bald

head of the man in front. I looked at a small child who was giving

her mother a hard time…

2. Underline all the **ld** words.

3. Say these **ld** words aloud.

bald	weld	mild	build	sold
gild	wild	scald	scold	head

4. Join the rhyming pairs in the words above.

5. Make up four sentences of your own, using **ld** words. Write them on the back of this sheet.

6. **Gild** is associated with **gold**. What might **to gild** mean? Use a dictionary to find the meaning and write it in your wordbank next to the word.

7. Read how the story continues.

Second instalment

The train raced on. There was no enjoyment in this trip. I couldn't

say anything more to Mum. I kept looking at things.

   'Government in trouble', I read in the newspaper alongside me.

'New equipment bought', was another heading.

   I tried to count the clickety-clacks that the train made, but it was

going too fast. The train began to slow down.

   "Can you hold on?" asked Mum.

   I did, and that was a mighty achievement, I can tell you!

8. Circle all the **ment** words in the story above.

The **ment** words you have
circled are nouns. They
become nouns by adding
ment to the verb. Knowing
this helps you to spell them.

9. Now look at these words.

Verb	Noun
install	instalment
enjoy	enjoyment
govern	government

10. What are the tricky parts of **instalment** and **government**? Write the words in your wordbank. Underline the tricky parts.

11. Make these verbs into nouns by adding **ment**. (Be careful of words ending in **y** – you will need to change the **y** to an **i**.) Write the new words below.

postpone _____   develop _____

arrange _____   accompany _____

measure _____   equip _____

12. Add any new words to your wordbank. Remember to Look–Say–Cover–Write–Check.

It's mine

An apostrophe can be used to show that a letter (or letters) have been left out.

For example: I'm = I am
                      he's = he is *or* he has

An apostrophe can also show that something is owned (or possessed). When something is owned, the apostrophe is usually placed after the last letter of the owner.

For example: The **athlete's** foot was blistered.

Ask yourself: Who owns the foot?
Answer: the athlete.
What is the last letter of the word **athlete**?
Answer: **e**.
So the apostrophe goes after the **e**.

Note: If the word is plural (for example, **athletes**), the apostrophe goes after the **s**.

1. Decide where the apostrophe should go in each of these sentences. Write the word with the apostrophe in the correct place. The first one has been done for you.

Bens favourite spot is the canal. $\underline{Ben's}$

Jades favourite sport is swimming.   _____

Gopals visit to the museum was fantastic.   _____

The five boys football sweaters were dirty.   _____

The familys favourite visit was to the local art gallery. _____

The families trip to the park was a disaster.   _____

The ladys horse jumped the hedge.   _____

The ladies horses jumped the hedge.   _____

Photocopiable 📖 S C H O L A S T I C Continued on ▶

Name

inued from P38

When a noun changes to form a plural without an **s**, such as the word **man** which becomes **men**, the apostrophe is placed after the last letter of the owner.
For example: the **men's** hats
Ask yourself: Who owns the hats?
Answer: the men.
What is the last letter?
Answer: **n**.
So the apostrophe goes after the **n**.

2. Decide where the apostrophe should go in each of these sentences. Write the word with the apostrophe in the correct place.

The childrens games are played in the park. _____

The womens club is near our house. _____

The mens cricket match was exciting. _____

The airmens squadron was famous. _____

The horsewomens skills were outstanding. _____

3. Read this passage. Put in apostrophes where you think they are needed.

Mr Jones team won the championship. Sigrids throw from the line

was the deciding goal. All of the girls friends and their families were

waiting outside the womens dressing room.

   "It is the teams win, not mine," Mr Jones said.

4. Now write three sentences of your own, using the apostrophe of possession with these nouns:

walker   spaceman   our class

_____

_____

_____

Name

toe	float	shoulder
whole	bald	
drive/drove	ride/ridden	dangerous
catch/caught	beautiful	
ship/shipped	swim/swimming	planned
tap/tapped	plan/planned	
enjoyment	healthy	honest
fastest	honour	
quarrelling	benefited	sighing
travelled	propelling	
knot	ghostly	ghetto
knuckle	knee	

Look at these words.

Say them aloud.

Cover each set of words.

Write them in your workbook.

Check to see if you are right.

When you have written each set of words, CHECK them to see if they are right. If they are right, put a tick. If any are wrong, cross them out. Look carefully at the correct word(s) again, note where you went wrong and write them again in your wordbank.

There are 37 words. How many did you get right first time?

Photocopiable   ■SCHOLASTIC Continued on

Name

1. While we were travelling, Nick and I played I-spy.

2. The bald-headed assistant tried to sell us some equipment for our study.

3. She made all the arrangements for the excursion to the circus.

4. I thought I would work out the measurements so that we could build it.

5. The men's feet were sweaty, but the ladies' feet were even sweatier!

6. Jack's knapsack had been used so much that it was totally useless.

7. The women's game of cricket was quite exciting and worth travelling some distance to see.

8. It was certainly an achievement when our team had the honour of receiving the first prize.

9. In spring, the cherry trees begin blossoming and look beautiful in the sunlight.

10. They searched for their brother on the mountain and eventually they found him.

Look at these sentences.

Say them aloud.

Cover each sentence.

Write them in your workbook.

Check to see if you are right.

Do the same with these sentences. (Don't forget to look at the punctuation!) You can WRITE, then CHECK after each sentence.

How many sentences were correct?

Enter any words that were not correct into your wordbank under the correct letter. Do this even if the word is there already.

Hovercrafts and headaches

 sk blends at the end of words are not very difficult to spell if you say the words before you write them.

1. Read this passage. Complete the **sk** words.

Holidays

When we go for a holiday, I a_____ Dad if we can go to the beach. I

like to ba_____ in the sun and swim until du_____. It's more fun than

hard ta_____s at my de_____ when I am at school. There is always

the ri_____ of sunburn, so I slip on my shirt, slop on the sun cream and

slap on my hat.

Many compound words apply to travel. The words **hovercraft** (hover + craft) and **motorbike** (motor + bike) are compound words.

2. Here are some more words which can be put together to make compound words. Join the words to make as many compound words as you can. Write them in your workbook.

| head | milk | book | play | ground | cook | ache |
| cup | shell | lunch | board | fish | shake | time |

3. Read these sentences, then write some of the compound words you have made in the spaces.

Mussels and oysters are _____.

Too much noise gives you a _____.

At _____ we sit in the _____.

I like to drink a _____.

In the kitchen there is a _____ and a _____.

tinued from P42

Unit **7**

4. Build these **oo** word families by finishing the words.

| o | oe | ue | ew | | ou |

d_____   sh_____   bl_____   br_____   f_____   y_____

t_____   can_____   cl_____   ch_____   scr_____

l_____se   s_____   dr_____   shr_____d

                                   tr_____   fl_____   sl_____

> Check the meaning of this word.

                                                     gr_____   thr_____

5. Fill in the spaces to complete the words with the **oo** sound. Choose from the words that you have made above.

I d_____ like travelling t_____ the country under the bright,

bl_____ sky. Usually I go by train but once I fl_____. What

d_____ y_____ d_____?

Give me a f_____ cl_____s!

D_____ you go by can_____?

You go by bike! How shr_____d!

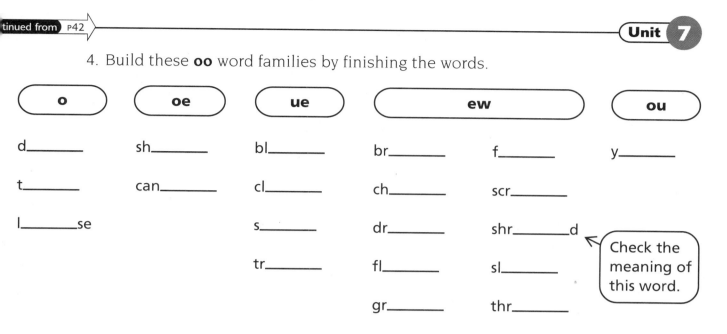

6. Complete these words with the **oo** sound, using the correct spellings.

bl_____   br_____   dr_____

tr_____   thr_____   f_____

cl_____   ch_____   cr_____

7. In your workbook, write four sentences of your own, including **o**, **oe**, **ue**, **ew** and **ou** words. Make sure they all have the **oo** sound.

Name

Objective: Add suffixes to words ending in e. Use regular past tense.

Unit 8

I'm amazed!

 When we add the suffix **ing** to words that end in **e**, we usually drop the **e**.
For example: advis**e**   advis**ing**

Past tenses need only **d** when verbs end in **e**.
For example: advis**e**   advis**ed**

1. Add **d**, then **ing** to these verbs. Write any new words in your wordbank.

advise   *advised*   *advising*   chase   _____   _____

amaze   _____   _____   complete _____   _____

amuse   _____   _____   damage   _____   _____

announce _____   _____   giggle   _____   _____

bake   _____   _____   hate   _____   _____

blame   _____   _____   include   _____   _____

bore   _____   _____   notice   _____   _____

capture   _____   _____   shape   _____   _____

cease   _____   _____   surprise   _____   _____

charge   _____   _____   wipe   _____   _____

2. Read these sentences, then complete them by writing some of the verbs you have made. Be careful to use the correct tense.

The children kept _____ every time they heard the funny noise.

The zoo-keepers were _____ the lion that had escaped; at

last they _____ it.

The fireworks made an _____ display.

Harry _____ all these scones by himself.

Photocopiable ◼ S C H O L A S T I C Continued on ▸
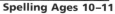

Name

Objective: Add suffixes to words ending in *y*, *w* or *x*.

ﾌued from P44

> Words that end in **y** (and have a consonant before the **y**) change the **y** to **i** before adding any suffix except **ing**.
> For example: **study** ends in **y** and has a **d** (a consonant) before the **y**.
> stu**dy**   stud**ied**   stud**ies**   study**ing**

3. Add **ed** or **ing** to these verbs. Write the new words below.

ed		ing	
accompany	_____	spy	_____
reply	_____	steady	_____
try	_____	study	_____
marry	_____	worry	_____

> Words that end in **w** or **x** simply add the suffix to the root word.
> For example: allo**w** allow**ed** allow**ing** allow**able** allow**ance**
>   fi**x**   fix**es**   fix**ed**   fix**ing**   fix**able**

4. Add **ed** and **ing** to these verbs. Write the new words below. The first one has been done for you.

ed	ing
fax _faxed_____	_faxing_____
mow _____	_____
mix _____	_____

5. Read these sentences, then fill in the spaces with some of the words you have made above. Make sure you use the correct tense.

He hasn't r_____ to my letter.

We keep w_____ about our old, sick dog.

My sister a_____ me to the disco.

6. Look carefully at these words. In your workbook, write four sentences of your own, using as many of the words as possible.

journey	journeyed	journeying	stray	strayed
straying	destroyer	destroy	destroyed	destroying

Objective: Spell *I* and *II* adjectives and adverbs.

Take care

The word **careful** means 'full of care'.
The word **graceful** means 'full of grace'.
When we add the suffix **full** to words in this way, we drop the last **I**.
care + full = care**ful**
grace + full = grace**ful** } adjectives

1. Add **ful** to these words. Write the new words. They are all adjectives.
(Remember what happens to the **y** in words ending in **y**.)

beauty_____   hope _____

event _____   wish _____

colour _____   wonder _____

When we add an **II** prefix to words, we also drop one **I**.
For example: we**ll** + fare = we**l**fare

Note that a**ll** + right = all right *or* a**l**right.
And a**ll** + together = all together *or* a**l**together.

3. Make new words from these word parts.

well + come _____   all + ready _____

skill + full _____   all + mighty _____

all + most _____

When we make adjectives into adverbs we often add **ly**.
For example: sad   sad**ly**

When we add **ly** to adjectives ending in **I**, we keep the **I**.
For example: He is a **careful** driver. (The adjective **careful** describes the noun **driver**.)

He drove **carefully**. (The adverb **carefully** describes the verb **drove**.)

Photocopiable ☛ SCHOLASTIC Continued on ▶

inued from P46

Unit 9

4. Make these nouns into adjectives and adverbs.

	adjectives	**adverbs**
beauty	_____	_____
care	_____	_____
hope	_____	_____
grace	_____	_____
colour	_____	_____
play	_____	_____

5. In your workbook, write one sentence for each of the adjectives and adverbs you have made above.

6. Read this story, completing the words with **l** or **ll**.

Our eventfu____ trip

The car went beautifu_____y when we started and Dad is a ski____fu____

driver. You cannot forete_____ what will happen, however, and something

rather scary did happen when we were a____most at our destination.

Dad had just turned off the motorway and was making his way carefu_____ towards

the sign for the old farmhouse where we were staying. We were all hopefu_____ of good

weather and were admiring the colourfu_____ flowers in the hedgerows.

Suddenly, as we approached the farmhouse, a mist came down; none of us could see

clearly. We hoped everything would soon be a_____right; instead, the mist thickened.

7. In your workbook, write two or three paragraphs to finish the story. When you have finished, swap your story with a partner and check each other's spellings and punctuation. You can then edit what you have written.

Name

Objective: Spell *advise, advice, practise* and *practice.*

Practice makes perfect

1. Read the following text. The **environment** refers to our surroundings – country or town.

The environment – we can all help

There's a lot of talk about damage to the environment these days. This includes the destruction of forests, ozone holes in the atmosphere and acid rain. Can you help save the planet? Environmental groups can advise you about many things you can do.

1. Recycle paper, bottles, plastic, cans and discarded clothes.

2. Start a compost heap to use up all your kitchen scraps.

3. Reduce the amount of rubbish you put out each week.

4. Try not to use products in spray cans.

5. Don't use toxic chemicals in the garden.

6. Be careful with the amount of electricity, gas and water you use.

Your family can practise good environmental habits that will help our planet. One more word of advice: by showing that these practices work, you can change others, so devise your plan and stick to it – our planet is worth saving.

When we write **advise** and **practise**, we are using them as verbs (**to advise, to practise**).

When we spell them with **ice** endings we are using them as nouns (**the advice, the practice**).

2. Try to extend the list of advice to ten points by adding your own ideas for helping the environment. Write them in your workbook.

3. Add new vocabulary to your wordbank. Remember to Look–Say–Cover–Write–Check. It may help you to spell **environment** if you split it into four syllables: **en vir on ment**.

Photocopiable ■ S C H O L A S T I C **Continued on**

Objective: Spell *advise, advice, practise* and *practice*. Spell words which have the prefixes *em, en, im* and *in*.

inued from P48

4. Read these sentences, then fill in the spaces, using **practice**, **practise**, **advice** or **advise**. Remember that **practise** and **advise** are verbs (doing words).

He _____s the piano every day.

She was too late for the netball _____.

Please _____ me on which road to follow.

They did not listen to his _____.

> The prefixes **em** and **en** sometimes mean 'to make' or 'to put into or on'.
> For example: the word **embitter** means 'to make bitter'
>   The word **encamp** means 'to put into camp'.

5. Guess the meanings of these words.

> encircle   entangle   encase   engulf

6. Now use a dictionary to check the meanings of the words. Add any new words, with their meanings, to your wordbank.

7. Read this passage, filling each space with an **en** or **em** word.

We drove all day, then _____ near the river. Many tall

trees _____ our tent. We took care not to

_____ the guy ropes.

> The prefixes **im** and **in** mean 'not'.
> For example: the word **impossible** means 'not possible'.
>   The word **insufficient** means 'not sufficient'.

8. Write these **im** and **in** words and their meanings in your wordbank. Remember to Look–Say–Cover–Write–Check.

> inadequate   impure   impractical   incredible

9. Now write six sentences of your own, using **em**, **en**, **im** and **in** words. Write them in your workbook.

Name

Objective: Spell words which have the prefixes *pre* and *contra*.

Unit 11

Be prepared

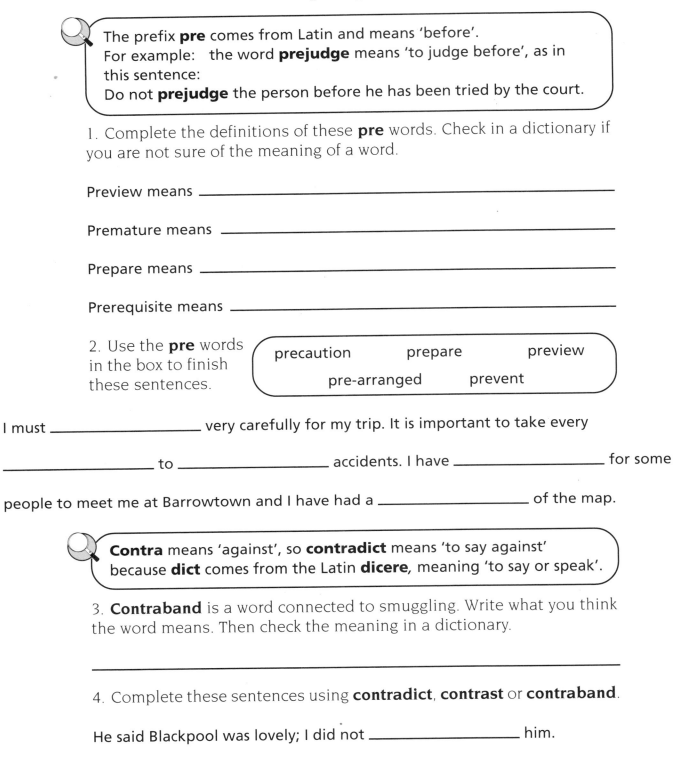

The prefix **pre** comes from Latin and means 'before'.
For example: the word **prejudge** means 'to judge before', as in this sentence:
Do not **prejudge** the person before he has been tried by the court.

1. Complete the definitions of these **pre** words. Check in a dictionary if you are not sure of the meaning of a word.

Preview means _____

Premature means _____

Prepare means _____

Prerequisite means _____

2. Use the **pre** words in the box to finish these sentences.

precaution	prepare	preview
	pre-arranged	prevent

I must _____ very carefully for my trip. It is important to take every

_____ to _____ accidents. I have _____ for some

people to meet me at Barrowtown and I have had a _____ of the map.

Contra means 'against', so **contradict** means 'to say against' because **dict** comes from the Latin **dicere**, meaning 'to say or speak'.

3. **Contraband** is a word connected to smuggling. Write what you think the word means. Then check the meaning in a dictionary.

_____

4. Complete these sentences using **contradict**, **contrast** or **contraband**.

He said Blackpool was lovely; I did not _____ him.

Smugglers brought _____ into the country.

Their black shirts _____ed with their white shorts.

Photocopiable ■ SCHOLASTIC Continued on

ued from P50

Words which have **gn** at the beginning do not sound the **g**. Words which have **mn** at the end do not sound the **n**.

5. Read these **gn** words.

gnome	**gn**arl	sovere**ign**
gnat	**gn**ash	**gn**u
rei**gn**	**gn**aw	

Check the meaning of this word if you are not sure of it.

6. Add any new words, with their meanings, to your wordbank, using Look–Say–Cover–Write–Check.

7. Say these **mn** words aloud.

hy**mn**   colu**mn**   autu**mn**   conde**mn**   sole**mn**

8. Now say these words aloud. Notice that in these words the **n** is sounded. Learning these words may help you to spell the root **mn** words.

hymnal   autumnal   condemnation   solemnity

9. Read these sentences, then fill in the spaces with **gn** or **mn** words.

I saw a _____ in the zoo. It is like an antelope.

On _____ days, many leaves on trees change colours.

A _____ is an old coin.

Our rabbit likes to _____ carrots.

The choir sang an ancient _____. They were very

_____.

The poor bear howled and began to _____ his teeth in agony.

Say it correctly!

If you say a word incorrectly you often write it incorrectly, too. For instance, if you say **chimley** instead of **chimney** you may write it the wrong way.

1. Say these words correctly, one by one. Look carefully at each word, then write it in your workbook. Say the word again as you write. Check to see if you are correct. Write the correct spelling of any words that you get wrong in your wordbank.

anything	(not anythink)
Arctic	(not Artic)
February	(not Febrey)
probably	(not proberly)
strength	(not strenth)
picture	(not pitcher)
clothes	(not cloves)
umbrella	(not umberella)
window	(not winda)
think	(not fink)
temperature	(not temprature)
particularly	(not particully)

2. Read this story aloud, taking care to pronounce the words clearly. Fill in the spaces with words from the list above.

In the winter month of Feb_____ we will

prob_____ travel to Spain where the t_____ is

higher. I cannot th_____ of any_____ better.

There is a house where we stay which has p_____y big

w_____s looking out on the beach. We can see all the

beach um_____s on the sand and people in swimming

costumes or light summer cl_____. When the sun is at

full st_____, it beats being in the Ar_____!

Name

Objective: Spell *sub* and *mar* words.

inued from P52

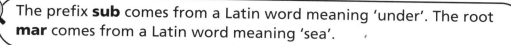

The prefix **sub** comes from a Latin word meaning 'under'. The root **mar** comes from a Latin word meaning 'sea'.

3. Read the following text.

Submarines

Submarines have been around longer than you realise. One of the earliest was built in 1776 in the USA. In modern vessels the environment is carefully controlled so that, whether in sub-zero or tropical waters, the crew can live quite comfortably on board the submarine.

Submarines sink or rise by making themselves heavier or lighter. Large tanks inside the hull are filled with sea water to make the submarine submerge. When the water is forced from the tanks using compressed air, the submarine rises to the surface.

The commander and his subordinates spend many months away from home on maritime expeditions.

4. Write out the text in your workbook. Add the word **submarine** to your wordbank. Underline the **sub** and **mar** parts of the word and write what each part means.

5. Here are some more **sub** and **mar** words. Read them aloud, then use a dictionary to check their meanings. Write any new words, with their meanings, in your wordbank.

subway	sub-editor
mariner	maritime
submit	submerge
marina	

Name

bask	risk	advice
dusk	shellfish	

Look at these words.

Say them aloud.

Cover each set of words.

Write them in your workbook.

Check to see if you are right.

study/studying	mow/mowing	reply/replied
practised	worry/worrying	
lose/losing	clue	shrewd
fly/flew	screw	
beautiful	beautifully	skilful
entangled	environment	
surprising	wiping	hating
giggling	amazing	
contraband	credible/incredible	prepare
precaution	practical/impractical	

When you have written each set of words, CHECK them to see if they are right. If they are right, put a tick. If any are wrong, cross them out. Look carefully at the correct word(s) again, note where you went wrong and write them again in your wordbank.

There are 38 words. How many did you get right first time?

Name

1. In autumn we attend football practice regularly.

2. The old men's hands were gnarled and their faces were wrinkled.

3. The ladies' clothes were probably bought from an expensive shop.

4. The mariners noticed that the submarine submerged gradually.

5. He announced the completion of the buildings he owned.

6. I was worried that the children's laughter would disturb the doctor.

7. The grocer ceased supplying them with provisions; they are hoping he will recommence soon.

8. Dad shouted, "Tread carefully – the ice may look welcoming, but it may crack quite suddenly."

9. I advise you to give thought to the environment; avoid using toxic chemicals in the garden.

10. She did not contradict me when I commented that the wedding was a solemn occasion.

Look at these sentences.

Say them aloud.

Cover each sentence.

Write them in your workbook.

Check to see if you are right.

Do the same with these sentences. (Don't forget to look at the punctuation!) You can WRITE, then CHECK after each sentence.

How many sentences were correct?

Enter any words that were not correct into your wordbank under the correct letter. Do this even if the word is there already.

Name

Objectives: Spell words with the *ow* sound as in *cloud*; spell words with *silent b* as in *doubt*.

Unit 13

To the mountains

1. Read these three paragraphs.

We live in Wales and in winter we often go to the mountains for a day. It's cold in the mountains but we walk and shout and soon get warm. Sometimes the clouds are so low that you can't see the valleys or the cliffs. It's just like fog all around.

Sometimes we go to a coffee lounge in the village and have a warm drink. They sell great chocolates there too. There's no doubt that they are the best chocolates ever. Some of them have hard centres, but others are so soft that they melt in your mouth.

The coffee lounge has a fountain in the window. The spouting water makes a sound like falling rain. People throw coins into the fountain. The owner collects the coins, counts them and then sends the money to the hospital in Cardiff.

2. Write one of the paragraphs in your workbook. Then write the words with the **ow** sound from all three paragraphs.

 Did you notice the **silent b** in **doubt**?

3. Read aloud these other **silent b** words.

| doubtful | climb | tomb | dumb | plumber | bomb |

4. Write the words in your wordbank. Use Look–Say–Cover–Write–Check. Don't forget to check the meanings of any words you don't know in your dictionary.

Objective: Spell words with *ow* sounds as in *crowd*, *cloud* and *show*.

5. Say these words aloud: (low   cow) Can you hear the difference?

The letters **ow** can be sounded in different ways.

6. Read these sentences aloud, then fill in the gaps with **ow** words. Listen for the different sounds **ow** makes.

Tie a b_____ in your hair.

Be very careful when you wash that mixing b_____l.

The brothers had a terrible r_____.

R_____, r_____, r_____ your boat.

I'll sh_____ you my drawings.

The singer b_____ed and then went behind the curtains.

The s_____ had six piglets.

His car was t_____ed away.

The cr_____ and the _____l are both birds.

The grass was m_____n so l_____ that n_____ it hardly sh_____s.

7. Now write the completed sentences in your workbook.

The **ow** sound, as in **cow**, is usually spelled **ou**.
For example: cl**ou**d

8. Read this list of definitions. Write the **ou/ow** word for each one.

a large dog	h_____	a dark colour	br_____
circular	r_____	a part of your gut	b_____
Put it on with a	p_____ puff.	a flat fish	fl_____
seen in the sky	cl_____	to die in water	dr_____
many people together	cr_____		

A stupid thing to do

1. Read this story.

In summer I go to the pool where we have our swimming carnival. Usually I have a swim and then run around on the grass. I always use a strong sunscreen lotion so I won't get sunburned.

One day I was very silly. I climbed up on to the high diving board and bombed into the pool below. I didn't see the little child swimming across the pool. When they dragged us both out of the pool, I had a broken thumb and he had a bleeding nose. I was lucky I didn't break any of his limbs.

It was a stupid thing to do.

2. Underline all the words in the story that have a **silent b** in them.

3. Now make some more **silent b** words. Read them aloud. Notice that **silent b** often comes after **m**. Remember the letter string **mb**.

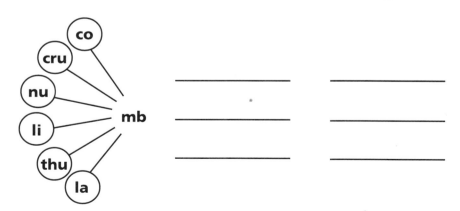

co
cru
nu
li
thu
la

mb

_____ _____

_____ _____

_____ _____

4. Write all the **silent b** words in your wordbank. Underline the **mb** in each word.

5. In your workbook, write five sentences, using **silent b** words.

Photocopiable ■SCHOLASTIC Continued on

Name

> When **ci** comes after a vowel, it sounds like **sh**.
> The ending **cian** sounds like **shun**.
> The ending **cious** sounds like **shus**.

6. Read these words aloud. Circle the **sh** sound in each word.

magician	suspicious
optician	technician
mathematician	precious
delicious	electrician
precocious	

7. Write any new words in your wordbank. Use Look–Say–Cover–Write–Check. Don't forget to check meanings of new words in your dictionary.

8. Read these sentences, then fill in the spaces with **ci** words from above.

The _____ tested my eyesight.

On a hot day, an ice cream tastes _____.

Kevin can do sums quickly; he is a great _____.

An _____ came to mend our television.

If children behave as though they are older than they really are, we say they are _____.

When I saw the door was open, I became _____.

9. Now write the completed sentences in your workbook. Try to write them from memory: look at the sentence, say it, cover it, write it, then check it.

Objective: Spell words which have the suffixes *sion* and *tion*.

Excursions and discussions

 The suffixes **sion** and **tion** make verbs into nouns.

verb	**noun**
discuss	discussion
celebrate	celebration

Only a few nouns end in **sion**.
- Verbs ending in **ss** give nouns ending in **sion**.

For example: expre**ss** – expres**sion**
- Verbs ending in **t** often give nouns ending in **sion**.

For example: admi**t** – admis**sion**
- Verbs ending in **d**, **de** or **se** often give nouns ending in **sion**.

For example: expan**d** – expan**sion**   divi**de** – divi**sion**
     revi**se** – revi**sion**

1. Make nouns from these verbs. Write them below.

   compress   extend   deride   precise

   _____   _____   _____   _____

2. Make these verbs into nouns. Take care! The rules above do not apply.

   practise   advise   ride   slide

   _____   _____   _____   _____

 Many nouns end in **tion**. To decide whether it is **sion** or **tion**, it helps to look at the little word in the big word.
For example: ac**t** – ac**tion**   discu**ss** – discu**ssion**

3. Read this poem aloud. Underline all the **sion** and **tion** words.

To go on an excursion

Is seldom any fun.

There's all that silly discussion

And nothing's ever done.

You have to get permission

To even scratch your nose.

It's a silly situation

The way excursions go.

4. Write any new **sion** and **tion** words in your wordbank, using Look–Say–Cover–Write–Check. Use a dictionary to check the meanings of any new words.

Photocopiable   ◼ S C H O L A S T I C Continued on

Name

inued from ▶ P60

Unit **15**

5. Make **sion** or **tion** words from these words.

admit _____   permit _____

complete _____   situate _____

depress _____   discuss _____

erode _____   expand _____

omit _____   impress _____

calculate _____   celebrate _____

submit _____   immerse _____

extend _____

illustrate _____

excavate _____

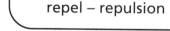

6. Add any new words to your wordbank. Don't forget to check the meanings.

7. Read these tricky **sion** and **tion** words.

compel – compulsion   satisfy – satisfaction
propel – propulsion   apply – application
expel – expulsion   compute – computation
repel – repulsion

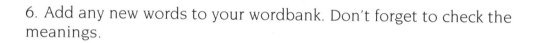

To learn how to spell tricky words:
● Say each word.
● Listen to the sounds it makes.
● Split it into syllables.
● Decide on the tricky part.
● Cover the word, and write it in your wordbank. Check!
● If you made a mistake, correct it, and look again at the word.
● Cover it, and write the word again. Check!

8. Write four sentences of your own in your workbook, using some of the tricky **sion** and **tion** words above.

Admirable adjectives

Adding **ible** or **able** to a word changes that word into an adjective.

Verb	Noun	Adjective
digest	digestion	digestible
apply	application	applicable

For example: People with poor **digestion** should eat **digestible** food.

This rule is applicable to most words.
able is more common than **ible** when used to form adjectives. If you are uncertain which suffix to use, you should check the spelling in your dictionary.

1. Add **able** to these words to make adjectives. Take care! Some of them are tricky. Try each word out first in your workbook and check it in a dictionary. Correct any errors, then write the words again below.

compare _____   work _____   change _____

reason _____   apply _____   depend _____

admire _____   inflame _____   expand _____

pass _____   drink _____   repute _____

excite _____   account _____   note _____

2. Write four sentences of your own, using adjectives that end in **able**.

_____

_____

_____

_____

Name

3. Here are some common adjectives ending in **ible**. Write the meaning for each one. The first one has been done for you. If you do not know what a word means, look it up in a dictionary.

audible   *able to be heard* _____

accessible   _____

credible   _____

edible   _____

flexible   _____

horrible   _____

invincible   _____

responsible   _____

sensible   _____

terrible   _____

visible   _____

4. Read these sentences, then fill in each space with an **ible** word from the list above.

The soldiers had never been beaten in battle. They seemed _____.

He sometimes tells lies, but this story is _____.

Although the biscuits were stale, they were _____.

In the distance, you could just about hear cars approaching;

as they came nearer they became more _____.

Plastic is more _____ than steel.

Leela's sister is very s_____ and r_____ for her age.

The castle is just _____ through the trees.

Stop and think

1. Read these words and underline the tricky parts.

beautiful	descend
entrance	gullies
information	journey
accommodation	pleasant
tour	sign

2. Now write them from *memory* in your wordbank. Remember to check your spellings!

3. Make some new words from these root words. The first two have been done for you.

accommodate	*accommodates accommodation accommodated accommodating*
enter	*enters entering entered entrance*
journey	
beauty	
please	
descend	
inform	
tour	
sign	

Photocopiable **M** SCHOLASTIC Continued on

Name

inued from P64

Abbreviations and contractions are the shortened forms of words. An **abbreviation** consists of the first, or the first and other letters of a word but does not have the final letter. An abbreviation is usually given a full stop, but not always.
For example:

vol.   (volume)
Jan.   (January)
NB   (note well – from the Latin **nota bene**)
PS   (postscript – from the Latin **post scriptum**)
RSVP   (please reply – from the French **Répondez, s'il vous plaît**)

A **contraction** consists of the first or the first and other letters of a word but ends with the same letters as the word. A contraction has no full stop.
For example: Mr   (Mister)
                 B'ham   (Birmingham)

5. Here are some abbreviations and contractions that are used frequently. Write the words from which they are derived. Use a dictionary to help you.

MP _____   am _____

Dr _____   FC _____

Mrs _____   pm _____

St _____   etc. _____

6. Write the abbreviations or contractions for each of these words and phrases.

Road   _____   Prime Minister   _____

British Summer   British
Time   _____   Broadcasting
                                         Corporation   _____
Bachelor of Arts   _____
                                         exempli gratia   _____
Please turn over   _____
                                         Very Important
Continued   _____   Person   _____

Name

Objective: Proof-read text to check for inaccuracies of spelling, punctuation and grammar.

Unit 18

Stanfield Bay

When we proof-read, we read writing very carefully, checking for errors. The errors can be:
- spelling mistakes
- punctuation mistakes
- mistakes in grammar.

It is very important that you learn how to proof-read your own writing and other people's writing, too.

1. Read this story. The spelling mistakes have been *underlined*, the punctuation mistakes have been *circled* and the mistakes in grammar have been *marked with a square*. Write your corrections above the text.

Last <u>Saterday</u> we went to Stanfield Bay. As we reached the top of

the hill above the <u>beech</u> we saw men and <u>wimmin</u> flying hang-

gliders. The hang-gliders jumped <u>of</u> the top of the hill, <u>glidded</u>

round and <u>finaly</u> landed on the <u>beech</u> below◯

We <u>desided</u> to watch them from the bay, so we drove down. From

<u>their</u> we we<u>|watch|</u> them <u>desend</u>◯They looked <u>butiful</u> as they soared

over the sea. It was <u>plesant</u> <u>whether</u> and it helped <u>there</u> flying.

Later, we walked <u>threw</u> the

old railway <u>tunel</u> and then we

had a <u>barbicue</u>. It was a

<u>wundafull</u> day!

2. Now write the passage correctly in your workbook.

Photocopiable ▲ SCHOLASTIC Continued on

Name

Objective: Use a thesaurus to find alternative, more interesting words.

:inued from P66

Unit 18

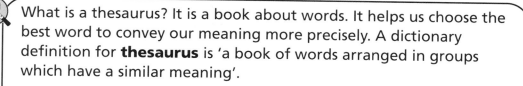

What is a thesaurus? It is a book about words. It helps us choose the best word to convey our meaning more precisely. A dictionary definition for **thesaurus** is 'a book of words arranged in groups which have a similar meaning'.

The word **thesaurus** comes from the Greek word **thesauros** which means 'treasure'. So we can think of a thesaurus as a treasure chest of words.

For example: The new bridge **crossed** the broad river.

Perhaps we could find a better word to use than **crossed**. Our thesaurus gives us four other words that mean 'crossed' and we can choose the one that is most appropriate. The words are **traverse**, **ford**, **bridge** and **span**.

Our thesaurus defines each word and these definitions help us to choose the word **span**.

Our sentence now says: The new bridge **spanned** the broad river.

3. Read these sentences. Use a thesaurus to find another word for the underlined word in each sentence. Remember to check the meanings of the words and to choose the most appropriate one. Write the new words above the text.

When she <u>got</u> to school, she played with her friend.

I <u>got</u> a present from my sister.

It is <u>nice</u> weather today.

I think this is a <u>good</u> book.

Name

Look at these words.

Say them aloud.

Cover each set of words.

Write them in your workbook.

Check to see if you are right.

powder	sign	doubt
shout	fountain	
excursion	division	action
permission	celebration	
hound	drown	tomb
round	comb	
immersion	satisfaction	digestible
situation	reasonable	
thumb	precious	magician
delicious	optician	
audible	descend	edible
terrible	accommodation	

When you have written each set of words, CHECK them to see if they are right. If they are right, put a tick. If any are wrong, cross them out. Look carefully at the correct word(s) again, note where you went wrong and write them again in your wordbank.

There are 30 words. How many did you get right first time?

Photocopiable ■ SCHOLASTIC Continued on

Name

1. The guests descended the stairs and went to the entrance of the house.

2. It was a beautiful day and our journey was quite wonderful.

3. On Saturday the workmen's tools had been left behind; we decided to return them.

4. She cried out, "Don't try to climb that mountain! I am doubtful whether the good weather will last."

5. The electrician came early and repaired our broken television.

6. They had a discussion about the excursion; some people thought it had been wonderful.

7. On the celebration of his birthday, we permitted him to use his new computer.

8. The dog was excitable and had a reputation for barking without reason.

9. The way through the woods was inaccessible, so we were sensible and returned from our journey.

10. The abbreviated form of **etcetera** is **etc**; the abbreviated form of **ante meridian** is **am**.

Look at these sentences.

Say them aloud.

Cover each sentence.

Write them in your workbook.

Check to see if you are right.

Do the same with these sentences. (Don't forget to look at the punctuation!) You can WRITE, then CHECK after each sentence.

How many sentences were correct?

Enter any words that were not correct into your wordbank under the correct letter. Do this even if the word is there already.

Objective: Spell words with *i* sounds as in *flight* and *height*.

Flight to Perth

1. Read this letter, then complete the **i** sound (as in **flight**) spellings.

Dear Pete,

We went to Perth in the plane as I said we would. It was a n_____t fl_____t and we

could see all the br_____t l_____ts of the city when we took off. What a s_____t!

I had a t_____t hold on my seat at first and I must admit I had a fr_____t when

the wheels went up with a bump. I gave a s_____ of relief when the Captain said that

we could unfasten our seat belts.

The plane travelled at a great h_____t and we could see the clouds below. It was a

really great fl_____t. I m_____t go again soon.

See you soon,

Carlos

2. Now write all the **i** words in alphabetical order.

_____

_____

3. Make more words that have the **i** sound as in **flight**. Write them below.
If there is a word you do not know, look up its meaning in your dictionary.

f
kn
bl ——— ight
pl
sl

_____

_____

_____

_____

_____

4. These **ight** words do not all have the same sound. Read them aloud.

delight	mighty	tight
nightingale	eight	weight

5. Now write four sentences, using **ight** words, in your workbook.

Photocopiable ■ SCHOLASTIC Continued on

Objectives: Spell words with *i* sounds as in *flight* and *height*; spell words with *ph* sounds as in *photograph*.

tinued from P70

Unit 19

The spelling of a word sometimes changes when it is used in a different way.

For example:
It is a catchy **tune**.	(noun)
She sings **tunefully**.	(adverb)
The playing was **tuneful**.	(adjective)
He **tuned** the piano.	(verb – past tense)

6. Read these sentences and write the correct words in the spaces. Three have been done for you.

I had a fr*ight*_____. (noun)

It was a fr_____ experience. (adjective)

Did you fr_____ that bird? (verb – present tense)

I was fr_____ by the loud noise. (verb – past tense)

It was a t*ight*_____ fit. (adjective)

I t_____ the nut with the spanner. (verb – present tense)

He t_____ the nut yesterday. (verb – past tense)

I heard a loud s*igh*_____. (noun)

I s_____ when I am sad. (verb – present tense)

I s_____ last week. (verb – past tense)

In **ph** words like **photograph** the letters **ph** sound like **f** as in **fan**.

7. Write these **ph** words in your workbook. Don't just copy! Use Look–Say–Cover–Write–Check.

| telephone | photograph | photography | elephant | triumph |
| orphan | dolphin | pheasant | phobia | |

Check what this word means.

8. Complete these sentences, using **ph** words.

She hated spiders; in fact her fear of them had developed into a _____.

A long-tailed bird flew out of the hedge; I thought it was a _____.

In the quagmire

There are two things to remember about the letter **q**. One is that it spells the **k** sound; the other is that it always appears with the letter **u**. Together they say **kw** as in **qu**ick.

Sometimes the letters **qu** are in the middle of a word, such as in ac**qu**ire, e**qu**ip and re**qu**est. The most common place is at the beginning, as in **qu**aint, **qu**ick and **qu**iz.

1. Read these **qu** words.

quail	quotation	quake	quiver	quiz	requiem
acquit	requisition	quite	quagmire	qualify	question
equip	equipment	quaint	quadruple	equinox	sequence
query	quote	equestrian	acquire	quiet	equate
sequin	equation	quality	quibble	quarantine	queue

2. Look at the beginning of each of the **qu** words above, then write the words in your workbook under these headings.

acqu	equ	que	qui	quo	requ	sequ

3. Fill in the missing spaces to complete the **qu** words and definitions. Remember to use a dictionary to check meanings.

equ_____	matching or the same
equ_____	a triangle with all sides equal
equilibrium	_____
requ_____	to need
sequ_____	a continuation of things
qu_____	a four-sided shape
qu_____	any four-footed animal
quarrel	_____
qu_____	where rocks and stone are mined
qu_____	half of a half

Photocopiable ■ SCHOLASTIC Continued on

Name

Objective: Spell words with *qu*.

4. Write any new **qu** words in your wordbank, using Look–Say–Cover–Write–Check. Remember to check meanings in a dictionary.

5. Read this passage, then fill in the spaces to complete the **qu** words.

> You re_____ire e_____ment of top _____ality
>
> to travel in Australia _____ickly and safely. You will be
>
> _____ite well e_____ipped if you ac_____ire a
>
> variety of light clothes and warm things for cold nights. Remember
>
> that parts of Australia are near the E_____ator. It is best to
>
> camp in _____iet spots. Have a great time!

The equinox occurs twice a year when the sun crosses the equator. Then the length of the day equals the length of the night. The word comes from the Latin words **aequus** (equal) and **nox** (night).

6. Write four sentences of your own, using these **qu** words. Add a suffix or a prefix to words if you need to. (For example: **quarrel** – **quarrelled**.)

quarrel	queue	quiet	quite

_____

_____

_____

_____

A tricky **qu** word is **quay**, which sounds like **key**.

7. Learn the tricky word **quay**. Write it in your wordbank.

Be silent!

The letters **g** and **k** are often silent at the beginning of words.
For example: **g**nome   **k**nee

1. Say the words in these word families. Listen to the sounds and look carefully at them. Write them in your workbook. Put any misspelled words into your wordbank. Make sure you know all their meanings.

g	k
gnarled	knapsack
gnash	knead
gnat	knee
gnaw	knit
gnome	knot
gnu	know
	knuckle

The letters **gn** and **kn** often go together. Look carefully at these letter strings and learn them.

2. Fill in each space with the correct **gn** or **kn** word.

A _____ is a South African antelope, often called a wildebeest.

Heidi couldn't pull the ring off her finger because it wouldn't go over her _____.

When Max came to the place where the wild things are they roared their terrible roars

and _____ their terrible teeth and showed their terrible claws.

There is a _____ in our garden. He is green and very small with a red pointed hat.

To _____ dough to make bread, you press and pull and turn it with your hands.

Most **silent p** words come from the Greek language. If you know the origin of a word (where it comes from and what its parts mean), you can often spell the word more easily.

For example: **pterodactyl** comes from the Greek words **pteron** (wing) and **dactylus** (finger). It was a flying reptile which had wing membranes supported by a finger. Say the word in syllables: **pter o dac tyl**.

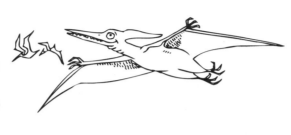

3. Split each of these **silent p** words into syllables. Say each word in syllables. Look carefully at each word. Cover each word. Then write each word in syllables.

> pneumatic

> pneumonia

_____

_____

> pseudonym

> psychology

_____

_____

4. Now write the **silent p** words in your wordbank in alphabetical order.

5. Read these definitions. Write the **silent p** word that each one defines.

> not your real name

ps_____

> a machine which breaks the road surface

pn_____ drill

> inflammation of the lungs

pn_____

> study of the human mind

ps_____

It's tricky

1. Say these tricky words. They are easy to spell if you say them correctly.

diamond	(not dimend)	government	(not goverment)
height	(not heighth)	library	(not libery)
particularly	(not particuly)	recognise	(not recernise)
sandwich	(not samich)	secretary	(not secertry)
temporary	(not tempory)	tired	(not tied)

2. Now practise spelling these words. Say each word again, cover it and write it in your workbook. Check! If it is wrong, cross it out and try again. Underline any parts you find tricky. Look carefully at the difficult parts.

3. These words also have difficult parts. Say the words carefully and correctly.

accommodation	(two **c**s; two **m**s)
address	(two **d**s; two **s**s)
breakfast	(two parts – **break/fast**)
bicycle	(two parts – **bi/cycle**)
dining	(one **n** only)
descend	(**silent c**)
engine	(an **e** at the end)
expense	(spelled with **s**, not **c**)
valleys	(not **ies** at the end)
journey	(**silent o**)

4. Look carefully at the tricky parts of each word. Cover the words one at a time and write each one in your workbook. Check! If you make a mistake, cross it out and try again. Now enter all the tricky words in your wordbank (even if they are already there) and underline the tricky part of each word.

If any of these words are especially tricky for you, think of a way to help you to remember how to spell them. Making up a memory sentence can help.

For example: An **add**er is in address.

At breakfast I **break** my overnight **fast**.

Objective: Spell irregular verbs when used in the past tense.

inued from P76

Unit 22

Some verbs change their basic spelling when they are in the past tense. They are irregular verbs. Regular verbs often just add **ed**. For example:

	present tense	past tense
regular verb	jump	jumped
irregular verb	catch	caught

5. Read this passage. The sentences all have irregular verbs in them. Fill in the spaces with the past tense of the verbs. The present tense of the verb is in brackets. The first one has been done for you.

I (catch) __Caught__ a fish last Sunday. I (bring) _____ it home to

Mum. She (freeze) _____ it so we could eat it later. Last time I didn't catch

any fish. I (buy) _____ some at the fish shop. I (give) _____

these fish to Mum, too. We (eat) _____ those fish straight away.

6. Add the irregular verbs (in the past tense) to your wordbank. Check your spellings!

Irregular verbs usually change again when we make them into past participles. Remember: past participles are words that go with **has**, **have** or **had**. For example:

present	past	past participle
I know	I knew	I (have) known

7. Read this passage, then fill in the past participles. The present tense of the verb is in brackets. The first one has been done for you.

Around Australia

We have (fly) __flown__ around Australia in a jet plane. It has (be) _____

great fun. I had (think) _____ it would be. We have (see) _____ .

all kinds of places. Sometimes we have hired a car and have (drive)_____ to

different tourist spots. We have (buy) _____ many souvenirs.

8. Write the irregular verbs that you have filled in above in your wordbank. Remember to check your spellings!

Objective: Differentiate homonyms from homophones and learn words in each category.

Lessen the load

 Homo comes from the Greek word **homos**, meaning 'same'.
Homonyms are words with the same spelling but different meanings. For example: a **staff** is a stick or pole; **staff** also means 'a group of workers'. Therefore, the word **staff** is a homonym.

1. Write two meanings for each of these homonyms in your workbook. Use a dictionary if you are not sure.

pole	well	bat
yield	band	patient

 Homophones are words which sound the same but have a different spelling and meaning.
For example: **threw** **through**

2. Write homophones for these words.

heir _____   bare _____   heard _____

sun _____   manor _____   vein _____

lesson _____   pain _____   doe _____

3. Read this passage. Choose the correct homophone from the brackets and underline it.

Getting ready to go

"I hope the (whether weather) is fine," Mum said. "It is against my (principals principles) to drive (threw through) (rain rein reign), (whether weather) you like it or (knot not). Remember when we (mist missed) the (rode road rowed) and ended up in a (creak creek)!"

"Well, I'm ready," said Dad. "I've (chequed checked) the (weight wait) of the van. You (seem seam) to have (throne thrown) everything (inn in) except the kitchen sink. We are not (allowed aloud) to carry (to two too) much. It is against the (lore law). I might have to (lesson lessen) the (load lode)."

Photocopiable **SCHOLASTIC** Continued on

Name

Objective: Recognise different homophones and know the correct spellings by looking at the context.

ued from P78

Unit 23

4. Read this passage. Choose the correct homophone from the brackets and underline it.

Rowing

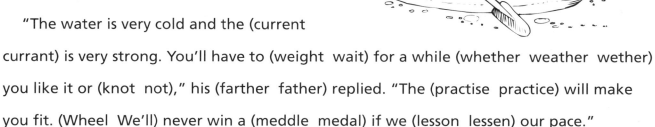

Ben had (rode rowed road) all morning and his (mussels muscles) were very (sore saw).

"How much (farther father) do we have (to two too) go?" he asked.

"The water is very cold and the (current currant) is very strong. You'll have to (weight wait) for a while (whether weather wether) you like it or (knot not)," his (farther father) replied. "The (practise practice) will make you fit. (Wheel We'll) never win a (meddle medal) if we (lesson lessen) our pace."

5. Replace the bold words in this passage with the correct homophones. Write in the spaces provided.

Keeping fit

"**Their** _____ are several **practises** _____ you must follow if you want to be fit and healthy," said the doctor. "If you **where** _____ a hat outside, you will **lesson** _____ the danger of skin cancer, **weather** _____ the sun is shining or not. And you must watch **you're** _____ **wait** _____. Eat plenty of **serials** _____, **course** _____ grain preferably, vegetables, fruit and lean **meet** _____, fresh fish or pulses. Exercise is important, **to** _____, and **sew** _____ is **wrest** _____."

6. How well did you do? Rewrite any sentences which were incorrect in your workbook.

7. Add any new words to your wordbank, with their meanings.

Name

Objective: Develop dictionary skills in order to find difficult words quickly.

Unit 24

Find it quickly

When you look for a word in a dictionary, you want to find it quickly. This may be difficult if the word begins with a silent letter or with a letter which can be spelled in two ways.
For example:
centre, **c**ircle, **c**elery and **c**eiling sound as though they begin with **s**

genius, **g**iant, **g**erm and **g**erbil sound as though they begin with **j**

phantom, **ph**oto and **ph**ysical sound as though they begin with **f**

To find a word in a dictionary, you may need to try different ways in which it might be spelled.

● An **s** sound at the beginning of words can be spelled **s** as in **s**ilver or **c** as in **c**ircus. These are the commonest spelling of the **s** sound.

Or **ps** as in **ps**eudonym (only a few words) and **sc** as in **sc**issors (very few words).

So if you are checking the spelling of a word with an **s** sound at the beginning, check **s** and **c** first, then **ps** and **sc**.

● A **j** sound at the beginning of words can be spelled **j** as in **j**ug or **g** as in **g**erbil. Both are common spellings. You need to try both letters if you are not sure.

● An **f** sound at the beginning of words can be spelled **f** as in **f**og or **ph** as in **ph**otograph. It is *usually* **f**, so check **f** first.

● An **n** sound at the beginning of words can be spelled **n** as in **n**ettle, **kn** as in **kn**ee, **gn** as in **gn**arled and **pn** as in **pn**eumonia. **n** and **kn** are the commonest ways to spell the **n** sound, so check these letters first. Then try **gn** and **pn**.

Name

nued from P80

1. Write the words which match these definitions. Guess the answer first, before you check in a dictionary. The first one has been done for you.

a very tall African animal with a long neck   _giraffe_

the title of a ruler in ancient Egypt   _____

a room underneath a building   _____

not your real name   _____

begins a game of tennis   _____

a painted canvas backdrop on stage   _____

a dwarf or goblin   _____

> If we know where words come from – their origins – it helps us to spell them and build more words.
>
> For example: the word **gymnast** comes from the Greek word **gumnastes**, one skilled in athletics. The hard part of the word is the beginning, **gym** (sounds like **Jim**). Other words like **gymnast** are **gymnastics** and **gymnasium**.

2. Use a dictionary to find the origin of each word below. Write it in your workbook. Then build one or two new words. One has been done for you.

gymnast   _gymnasium_   ski   _____
          gymnastics   _____

agile   _____   strong   _____

      _____

athlete   _____   swim   _____

      _____   _____

Name

Look at these words.

Say them aloud.

Cover each set of words.

Write them in your workbook.

Check to see if you are right.

flight	eight	straight
relief	delight	
acquire	knuckle	gnarled
pterodactyl	pneumatic	
tightened	telephone	phobia
frightened	photograph	
breakfast	government	tired
have bought	athletics	
queue	quickly	quarter
equipment	equator	
bicycle	address	physical
engine	caught	

When you have written each set of words, CHECK them to see if they are right. If they are right, put a tick. If any are wrong, cross them out. Look carefully at the correct word(s) again, note where you went wrong and write them again in your wordbank.

There are 31 words. How many did you get right first time?

Photocopiable ◀SCHOLASTIC Continued on

Name

1. The aeroplane flew at a great height and I sighed with relief when the flight was over.

2. He was terrified of rats and snakes; many other people have the same phobia.

3. The electrician prepared his equipment so that he could repair our telephone.

4. Because parts of Australia are near the equator, you will require clothes which are light and easy to wear.

5. An equestrian is someone who enjoys riding horses; often they like to qualify for competitions.

6. A gnu is a South African antelope which is sometimes called a wildebeest.

7. The doctor travelled to see the girl who was suffering from pneumonia.

8. Members of Parliament (MPs) are men and women chosen by the people to form our government.

9. They have flown around Australia, driven to different tourist areas and bought many souvenirs.

10. The gymnasts were extremely agile and practised in the gymnasium every day.

Look at these sentences.

Say them aloud.

Cover each sentence.

Write them in your workbook.

Check to see if you are right.

Do the same with these sentences. (Don't forget to look at the punctuation!) You can WRITE, then CHECK after each sentence.

How many sentences were correct?

Enter any words that were not correct into your wordbank under the correct letter. Do this even if the word is there already.

Name

Objective: Spell words with *oy* sounds as in *boy* and *boil*.

Unit 25

A trip overseas

1. Read this passage. Underline all the **oy** sounding words.

There are many ways to travel overseas. The most common choice is to fly.

Flying is quick and enjoyable, although you can get a seat alongside some annoying passengers. They can almost spoil your trip, so it is wise to avoid them if you can. On my first trip, I sat alongside a very nice boy. He was very quiet and made no noise throughout the flight. He read most of the time.

Another way to travel is to take a sea voyage. This was the way my grandma and grandpa went overseas. My grandma says it's the best way because it's slow and relaxing and there are always lots of things to do. Everyone joins in to have a good time. The only thing that spoilt it for her was the oily smell of the engines. Their first overseas trip was on a ship called the *Royal Trader*.

2. Make **oil** words from the letters in this grid. Write the words below.

	b	c
f	oil	
sp	t	s

_____   _____

_____   _____

_____   _____

Name

Objective: Spell words with *ur* sounds.

inued from P84

Unit 25

3. These groups of words all contain **ur** sounds. Add one more word of your own to each group.

ur	ir	er	ear	or
fur	stir	kerb	learn	doctor
burn	shirt	verb	rehearse	inspector

_____ _____ _____ _____ _____

4. Complete these words by writing in the correct **ur** spelling.

h_____b   k_____nel   n_____se   f_____ther

w_____ld   l_____n   th_____mal   w_____m

_____th   sup_____ b   w_____th

5. Now complete these sentences with words that all have an **ur** sound.

What a sup_____b lunch!

You have to be al_____t and _____ly if you want to catch the w_____m.

Do you have enough n_____ve to dive into the s_____f?

The actors l_____ned their parts at reh_____sal.

6. Write five sentences of your own in your workbook, using these **ur** words. Use a dictionary to check the meaning of any new words.

immerse	surplus	swerve	worth	purchase

7. Write these **ur** words in your wordbank. Don't forget to Look–Say–Cover–Write–Check.

superb	earth	hurl	worse
world	learn	further	nurse

Photocopiable ■ SCHOLASTIC

Scholastic Literacy Skills
Spelling Ages 10–11   85

Objective: Learn compound words.

Let's stay together

We often join words to make a new word. It helps us to spell that new word if we know how to spell the smaller words that combine to make it.
For example: **showerproof = shower + proof**

1. Read these words. Break them up into two smaller words within each word and write them below. The first one has been done for you.

airport   *air*   *port*   suitcase   _____ _____

passport   _____ _____   backpack   _____ _____

toothpaste _____ _____   handbag   _____ _____

ballpoint   _____ _____   sunburn   _____ _____

toothbrush _____ _____   seasick   _____ _____

laptop   _____ _____   headache   _____ _____

2. Complete this story, using the words above.

Travelling abroad

We arrived at the _____ and checked-in at the desk. The officials

checked our tickets and our _____s, weighed our s_____

and b_____s and gave us boarding passes. In my h _____ I

had my s_____ pills, my _____ cream, a tube of

_____, and a few tablets in case I developed a h_____. I also

had my _____ and a _____ pen in the bag. I saw one lady

carry on her l_____ computer.

     We finally went through Customs and gathered in the flight lounge. In a

short time they called the flight and we boarded the aeroplane.

Photocopiable ▶ SCHOLASTIC Continued on

Name

inued from P86

Sometimes we confuse words in our writing because they sound the same (homophones).

For example: **here** and **hear** are homophones. They sound the same but mean different things.

I live **here**.

I can **hear** the bells ringing.

3. Look up these pairs of words in your dictionary. Find out how they differ, then write the words and your own definition for each in your wordbank.

read	straight	right	principal
reed	strait	write	principle

4. Read these sentences aloud, then write the correct words in the spaces.

The players went _____ into the showers after the match.

Are you going to _____ a letter to your uncle?

The _____ of the college is Dr Anne Ward.

She never shops on Sunday; it is against her _____s.

You are quite _____, as usual!

There is a _____ bed at the edge of the pond.

A narrow strip of water connecting two areas of water is called a _____.

Joke

Knock! Knock!

Who's there?

Francis.

Francis who?

France is on the other side of the Channel!

Objective: Spell *wh* words.

Remember the 'h'

wh words can be tricky to spell because often we do not sound the **h**.

1. Read these **wh** words aloud, taking care to sound the **h** in each word.

when	whistle	whale	whisper	white
whist	whip	whet	whiskers	whippet
whimper	wheels	wheat	whirl	whisk

2. Use a dictionary to check the meanings of any new words. Then write the words, with their meanings, in your wordbank.

3. Complete this grid of **wh** words and their definitions. Choose from the list of words above to fill in the right-hand column. The first one has been done for you.

definitions	wh words
to lash or flog	whip
vehicles run on them	
	whippet
the largest sea-animal	
	white
to speak very softly	
to turn round swiftly	
to cry with a whining sound	
	wheat
	whiskers
	whistle
at what time?	
to stimulate someone's appetite	

Photocopiable ▪ SCHOLASTIC Continued on

Objective: Spell *tch* words.

inued from P88

4. Read these **tch** words aloud. Use a dictionary to check the meanings of any new words.

watch	match	satchel	patch	ditch	scratches
fetch	catch	stitch	latch	hutch	kitchen

5. Complete this grid of **tch** words and their definitions. Choose from the list of words above to fill in the right-hand column. The first one has been done for you.

definitions	tch words
bring	*fetch*
used to be carried by schoolchildren	
the room where you cook	
	catch
an instrument for measuring time	
a piece sewn or stuck on	
	match
relief for an itch	
	hutch
a loop of thread	
a trench for drainage	
fastens a door shut	

6. Now write two sentences of your own, using **wh** words, and two sentences using **tch** words.

_____

_____

_____

_____

Name

Objectives: Spell tricky words which have silent letters; spell words with *ant* and *ent* endings.

Unit 28

Oh crumbs!

1. Read these tricky words. Underline all the silent letters.

crumb	lamb	subtle	science	Christmas	hour
wheat	thyme	spaghetti	raspberry	foreign	salmon

2. Check the meanings of any new words in a dictionary. Add the words with their meanings to your wordbank.

3. Read these sentences, then fill in the spaces to complete the silent letter words. Choose from the words above.

_____berry jam is my favourite.

The lam_____s were born in the spring.

T_____me is a herb with a su_____le flavour.

The word spag_____ comes from Italy, a fore_____ country.

She wiped the c_____s off the table.

4. In your workbook, write two sentences of your own, using silent-letter words.

 There is no hard and fast rule to help you choose between **ant** or **ent** endings. Grouping the words into 'family endings' may help you remember which words have which ending.

5. Look carefully at these two groups of words. They are organised by their family endings. Add two more words to each family ending group.

fragr**ant**   abund**ant**   import**ant**   _____   _____

excell**ent**   magnific**ent**   perman**ent**   _____   _____

6. Look–Say–Cover–Write–Check any new words and their meanings and add them to your wordbank.

7. Write four sentences in your workbook, using words ending in **ant** or **ent**.

Photocopiable ■ SCHOLASTIC Continued on

The consonant blends *lt* and *mp* occur in the middle or at the end of words.

8. Add **lt** or **mp** to the spaces to make words.

she_____er   sa_____ed   me_____ing   bo_____ed

pou_____ry   si_____le   bu_____ing   gui_____y

te_____erature   ca_____ing   ju_____er   tra_____

mou_____ing   gru_____y   pe_____ed   pi_____le

9. Read this poem aloud.

Rainstorm

Helter, skelter,
run for shelter,
bolt out of the rain.
Don't get grumpy,
damp and frumpy,
or you'll be a pain.
It's like camping,
simple tramping,
through the hills and plains.

Gregory Blaxell

10. Read it again to yourself, then cover it and try to write it from memory in your workbook.

11. Write words that rhyme with these words. The first one has been done for you.

quilt   *guilt* _____   melt _____   bump _____

colt _____   lamp _____   stamp _____

welter _____   lump _____   rump _____

Name

Objective: Listen to correct pronounciation of words in order to spell them correctly.

Unit 29

Don't leave it out

We misspell some words because we mispronounce them by leaving out sounds.
For example: should ⌒have
We do not say the **h**. In fact we often say **of** instead of **have**.

1. Here is a list of words we often mispronounce. The letters (and the sounds they make) that are commonly left out are circled. Say each of these words, and make sure you pronounce the circled letters.

Arctic	February	January	particularly	secretary	tired
clothes	government	library	probably	strength	violet
diamond	honorary	nearly	recognise	temporary	

Splitting words into syllables can help you to say them correctly.
For example: **incident = in ci dent**

2. Read the words again, using this list. Use the way the words are broken up into syllables to help you to say them correctly.

Arc tic	Feb ru ary	Jan u ary	par tic u lar ly	sec ret ary	tir ed
clo thes	gov ern ment	lib r ary	prob ab ly	streng th	vi o let
di a mond	hon or ary	near ly	rec og nise	tem por ary	

3. Now write the words in your wordbank. Use Look–Say–Cover–Write–Check.

4. Without copying the words above (cover them with a piece of paper), fill in the tricky part of each word.

Anta_____tic   li_____ry   st_____n_____th

d_____mo_____d   n_____ly   tem_____a_____y

Febr_____y   part_____la_____ly   t_____d

gov_____m_____t   pro_____ly   v_____l_____t

hon_____ry   re_____o_____n_____e

Jan_____ry   secre_____y

Name

Objective: Listen to correct pronounciation of words in order to spell them correctly.

inued from P92

Unit 29

5. Read these sentences, then fill in the spaces to complete the tricky words. Try to write the tricky words from memory, but check your spelling carefully.

The North Pole is within the A_____ Circle.

The girl put new c_____ on to come to school.

D_____s, emeralds and rubies are precious jewels.

Whichever political party wins the election becomes the g_____.

He held the position of H_____ Treasurer.

A l_____ is a place where we find information and books.

It's ne_____ time to go to bed.

I'm par_____ fond of chocolate.

He will pro_____y calm down soon.

Can you rec_____ him from the photo?

My mum's sec_____ is very intelligent.

The advertisement said it was a tem_____ position.

Do you get ti_____d at night?

The colours of the spectrum are red, orange, yellow, green, blue, indigo

and v_____.

Limericks are short, usually funny poems. The rules for writing them are quite simple: the first, second and fifth lines rhyme. The third and fourth lines rhyme. But they are not easy to write!

6. Read this limerick aloud.

The butcher

A careless young butcher called Fred
Cut his finger and watched as it bled.
He said, quite dismayed,
As the wound he displayed:
"I didn't know blood was so red."

Gordon Winch

Just for fun!

7. Try writing a limerick of your own. Remember to follow the rules!

Name

Many things

 Multi comes from the Latin word **multus**, which means 'many'. The Greek prefix **poly** also means 'many'. That is why, in English, the prefixes **multi** and **poly** both mean 'many'.
For example: **multi**ply – to make many
                        polygon – a many-sided object

1. Write these words in your wordbank and guess their meanings.

> multi-purpose   multicoloured   multiracial   multitude

2. Use a dictionary to check the meaning of each word. Correct your guesses if they were not quite right.

3. Read these sentences. Choose a **multi** word which makes sense for each space.

Scissors can be used for many things; they are _____.

There was a _____ of people at the festival.

The UK is a _____ country; many nationalities live here.

For the carnival, we put up _____ flags in the town.

 Semi comes from the Latin **semi**, which means 'half'.
For example: **semi**circle – half a circle

4. Write these words in your wordbank and guess their meanings.

> semi-detached   semiquaver   semi-final   semicolon

5. Now check the meanings in a dictionary. Correct your guesses if they were not quite right.

6. Write four sentences of your own in your workbook, using **semi** words.

Photocopiable ■ SCHOLASTIC Continued on

Name

Objective: Spell words with the prefixes *tele*, *mono* and *mal*.

Tele comes from Greek and means 'far off' or 'from afar'.

7. Read this passage, then circle all the **tele** words.

Nearly an overseas trip

The Olympic Games was televised direct from Sydney in 2000. We had very good telecommunication links with Australia, so the telecast was excellent. Telephones, telegraphs, telegrams, telexes and teleprinters were used to cover all the events.

    Many photographers also followed the events. They used telephoto lenses to get close-up shots of the athletes. Watching the Olympic Games on television was the closest thing I had to an overseas trip.

---

8. Use a dictionary to find the meaning of any word you are uncertain of.

9. Find out what these two words mean. Then write the words, with their meanings, in your wordbank.
    (telepathy   telescope)

10. Write two sentences, one using the word **telepathy** and the other using the word **telescope**.

_____

_____

Mono also comes from Greek and means 'one'.
For example: **mono**cycle – a one wheeled bike
               bicycle   – a two wheeled bike

Mal comes from the Latin **male** and means 'ill' or 'badly'. It's like the prefixes **ill** and **dis**.
For example: **mal**content, **dis**content – not content
               maltreat, **ill**treat – not to care for or not to treat well

11. Find out the meanings of these words, using a dictionary. Write each word and its meaning in your wordbank.

(monotone   malnutrition   monolith   malpractice)

12. Write four sentences of your own in your workbook, using **mal** words.

Name

Look at these words.

Say them aloud.

Cover each set of words.

Write them in your workbook.

Check to see if you are right.

thermal	malnutrition	shirt
spoilt	learn	
whistle	scratches	foreign
crutches	kitchen	
burn	rehearse	worth
worm	swerve	
hour	permanent	guilty
subtle	important	
toothpaste	melting	whisper
airport	straight	
building	semi-detached	semi-final
temperature	multicoloured	

When you have written each set of words, CHECK them to see if they are right. If they are right, put a tick. If any are wrong, cross them out. Look carefully at the correct word(s) again, note where you went wrong and write them again in your wordbank.

There are 30 words. How many did you get right first time?

Photocopiable **SCHOLASTIC** Continued or

1. On Wednesday the teachers displayed all types of books in the children's library.

2. The team wore strange outfits of violet covered with imitation diamonds.

3. Their secretary recognised the man who had nearly robbed them of all their money.

4. The diversion signs on the motorway are supposed to be temporary; that was eight months ago!

5. The girls sang cheerfully even though they had slept particularly badly.

6. There is a division of opinion regarding whether or not we should have had a bonfire.

7. The decision to purchase a football strip for the school received a cheer.

8. Since I had a headache, I thought it better to wait a while before going skating.

9. "That was an excellent lunch," he exclaimed, "my favourite food has always been salmon!"

10. A multitude of multicoloured kites suddenly appeared in one of my nightly dreams.

Look at these sentences.

Say them aloud.

Cover each sentence.

Write them in your workbook.

Check to see if you are right.

Do the same with these sentences. (Don't forget to look at the punctuation!) You can WRITE, then CHECK after each sentence.

How many sentences were correct?

Enter any words that were not correct into your wordbank under the correct letter. Do this even if the word is there already.

Thirsty work

Words with **ur** sounds are not *always* spelled with an **ur**. They can be spelled many ways.

1. Read these **ur** words aloud.

Thursday	murder	pursue	murmur
Saturday	burglar	purpose	turquoise

2. Read these words with **ur** sounds. Underline the letters which make the **ur** sound in each word.

journey   rehearse   first   superb   worse

3. Finish the spelling of these words with **ur** sounds.

m_____ky   c_____ve   c_____tsy

h_____dle   s_____ch   pref_____

th_____st   imm_____se   sub_____b

4. Complete this grid of definitions and words with **ur** sounds. Choose from the words above to fill in the right-hand column. The first one has been done for you.

definitions	words with 'ur' sounds
a greenish-blue colour	turquoise
	murmur
to chase or follow	
	rehearse
dark and gloomy	
	hurdle
to dip into liquid	
aim or intention	
	worse

Photocopiable   ■ SCHOLASTIC   Continued or

Name

inued from P98

5. Read the words in the satellite.

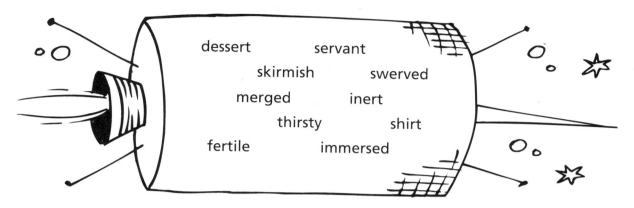

dessert   servant
skirmish   swerved
merged   inert
thirsty   shirt
fertile   immersed

6. Choose from the words above to fill in the spaces.

I had chocolate layer cake for_____.

I'm so _____ I could drink a well dry!

I fell into the river and went right under; I was completely _____.

The two roads _____ into one.

When we were at the castle the _____ brought morning tea.

A _____ is a small battle.

_____ describes something which does not move or do anything.

Do you wear a space _____ under a spacesuit?

He _____ to miss the meteor in his path.

You could see that it was a _____ planet by the fact that so many things were growing there.

7. Check that you can spell these ten words. Write them in your wordbank, using Look–Say–Cover–Write–Check.

skirmish	inert	shirt	swerved	fertile
dessert	thirsty	immersed	merged	servant

8. Now use six of the words above to write four or more sentences in your workbook.

Objective: Spell words with the schwa
suffix: *er, or, ar, re.*

Explorers

When we say the word **explorer** in ordinary speech, we do not
pronounce the **er** fully, as we do when we say a word like **her**. Instead,
we say something like **uh – explor/uh**. This final sound is called the
schwa and it is found in the pronunciation of many words in English.

1. All these words end in a schwa. Say them first, then underline all the
schwa sounds. The first one has been done for you.

ancest<u>or</u>	radiator	sculptor	solicitor	survivor	fibre
victor	burglar	grammar	scholar	vicar	metre
vinegar	disaster	explorer	gardener	player	theatre

_____   _____

2. Add two more words to the list of schwa words above.

3. Read this passage, then fill in the spaces with schwa words.

Attention space explor_____s!

Be a space explor_____, a travell_____ to the moon in my *Lun_____ Starship II*.

Passeng_____s will observe the behavi_____ of particul_____ planets, including

Jupit_____, and be amazed at the sight of the world at the equat_____ on the return

journey. There is no other space travel package of this calib_____ offered as a

regul_____ service to passeng_____s. You will have a personal conduct_____ and

announc_____. Join with us and become a conquer_____ of space.

Watch out for tricky words which have silent letters.
For example: colum**n** (**silent n**) s**c**ience (**silent c**) hi**gh** (**silent gh**).
The best way to learn how to spell these words is to remember what
the tricky parts look like.

4. Say these words aloud
and look carefully at them.
Underline the tricky parts.

column	hymn	autumn	abscess	adolescent
scent	science	scissors	neighbour	weigh

Photocopiable ▪ SCHOLASTIC Continued on

Name

Objective: Spell words with silent letters *n*, *c* and *gh*.

ued from P100

Unit 32

5. Write each word in your wordbank, using Look–Say–Cover–Write–Check. Did you spell the tricky parts correctly? If not, try the word again.

6. Read these sentences, then fill in the spaces to complete the tricky words.

It is because of s_____ce that we have been able to travel in space.

An ad_____ent is a teenager.

Nelson's Col_____ is in London.

You are big for your age. How much do you we_____?

8. Build onto these silent letter words. Say each new one as you make it. What do you notice about the **silent n**? Write the words below.

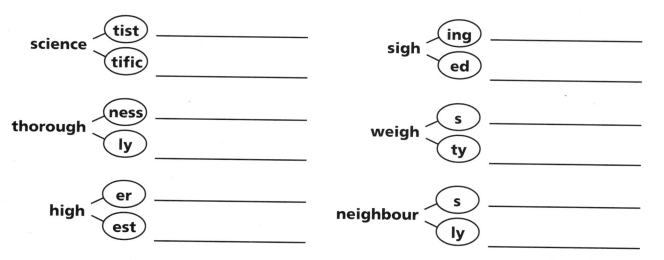

9. Build more new words from these tricky words. Say each new word as you make it and then write the new words below. Take care – you will have to drop letters in one of them.

10. Remember to check the meanings of any words which are new to you. Write their meanings next to the words in your wordbank.

Name

Objectives: Revise rules to help with spelling: adding suffixes (dropping the final *e*; retaining the *e* when adding *able*; doubling the final consonant); using *ice* or *ise*, as in *practice/practise*.

Unit 33

Drop it or double it

 When we add a suffix that starts with a vowel to words which end in **e**, we drop the final **e**.
For example: nurse + ing = nur**sing**

1. Add the suffixes to these words. Say each word aloud, then write the new words below.

serve + ant _____   telephone + ist _____

compute + ing _____   seize + ure _____

supervise + or _____   drive + ing _____

Take care with the suffix **able**. Remember these:
    notice + able = notic**ea**ble   manage + able = manag**ea**ble
    service + able = servic**ea**ble
When we add a suffix that starts with a vowel to words with consonant–vowel–consonant (CVC) endings, we double the final consonant before we add the suffix.
For example: pot + er = po**tt**er   travel + ing = trave**ll**ing

2. Add the suffixes to these words.

fit + er _____   sit + er _____   shovel + ed _____

fun + y _____   jewel + er _____   towel + ing _____

tan + ing _____   barrel + ed _____

ice at the end of a word means that the word is a noun. **ise** means that the word is a verb.
For example:
I went to football prac**tice**. **Practice** is the noun in this sentence.
I prac**tise** the piano. **Practise** is the verb in this sentence.

3. Choose the correct word from the brackets and write it in the space.

I go to netball (practise, practice) _____.

I try to (practise, practice) _____ at home, too.

Do you have a driver's (licence, license) _____?

Photocopiable **M** SCHOLASTIC Continued on

Name

tinued from P102

When we make words ending in a *consonant* + **y** into plurals, we change the **y** to **i**.
For example: la**dy** – lad**ies**   nan**ny** – nann**ies**.
But if the word ends in a *vowel* + **y**, it keeps the **y** in the plural.
For example: pull**ey** – pull**ey**s   k**ey** – k**ey**s

4. Complete these sentences, making the words in brackets plural.

The two (valley) _____ were very much the same. Both of our (journey) _____

took us through them. On these expeditions everyone carries (supply) _____ of food.

'**i** before **e** except after **c**' is a useful rule for many words.
But remember there are some words which do not follow it. We call them **exceptions to the rule**.
These are some of the words that follow the rule:
   bel**ie**ve   fr**ie**nd   f**ie**ld   rec**ei**ve   dec**ei**ve   c**ei**ling
These are some of the exceptions to the rule:
   th**ei**r   h**ei**ght   w**ei**ght   w**ei**rd   s**ei**ze

5. Complete these sentences, adding **ei** or **ie** words.

It was a great ach_____ment to get the job. It must have been a thrill to

rec_____ the letter. I saw you read it on the playing f_____ld. You let out

a loud shr_____k.

If you hear the sound **k** (or **hard c**) at the end of a word that has *more* than one syllable, the **k** sound is nearly always spelled with a **c**.
For example: pani**c**   toni**c**   criti**c**
One-syllable words that end with the **k** sound nearly always end in **ck**.
For example: du**ck**   bri**ck**   lo**ck**   sa**ck**
Words that have one syllable and a long vowel sound nearly always end in **k**.
For example: hoo**k**   boo**k**   bea**k**   spea**k**

6. Read these sentences, then fill in in the gaps with **c**, **ck** or **k**.

When the bri_____ came through the window, I was in such a pan_____

I could hardly l_____ at the damage.

Beth too_____ the sa_____ of rubbish to the tip.

Name

Be innovative

New words pass into our language all the time. We need new words to express new ideas and to give names to new inventions. We call these new words **neologisms**.
For example: The words **microwave** and **facsimile** are two neologisms. The words were 'invented' to name two new inventions.

1. Read this passage, then circle all the neologisms you can find. Look up the meaning of any word or phrase you are unclear about in a dictionary.

This new technology

Television plays a very important part in our lives. This box of integrated, transistorised circuits delivers us news, films, docudramas, soaps, sport and quiz shows. These days you do not need to get up from your settee to answer the phone, which may be cordless or cellular. You can integrate your phone, your TV and your computer and send and receive signals by using a modem.

Telecommunications technology is making giant leaps forward. Cellular phones use the mobile net framework. Even public telephones can be either payphones or phonecard phones. If you're on a boat, you can tap into the mobile net system on your VHF seaphone. Most of this is possible because of microchip technology. If you are lucky enough to have money in the bank, you can withdraw it at your local cashpoint machine.

If you're still bored, you can play computer games. The most advanced of these let you experience virtual reality.

And when you get hungry after all this activity and you want to eat in a hurry, try fast food outlets, or use a microwave or fan oven.

2. Write any new words and their meanings in your wordbank.

Photocopiable **SCHOLASTIC** Continued on

inued from P104

Objective: Spell neologisms.

3. Here are some more neologisms. Read them first, then check the meaning of any you are unsure about. Write the meaning of each word below.

telethon _____

polygraph _____

digital _____

compact disc player _____

mindset _____

4. Now write five sentences in your workbook to show you understand the meaning of the neologisms above.

Space exploration is a relatively new activity for humans, so it is not surprising that there are many new space words or old words that take on new meanings.

5. Read these two groups of word parts. Join the parts to make some new space words and write them in the rocket.

space	naut
super	sonic
astro	craft
space	computer
cosmo	rocket
retro	down
count	suit
micro	naut

6. Read this passage, then fill in the spaces with some of the new words you have created.

Ten, nine, eight, seven... the count_____ was nearly complete. The

_____nauts sat in their space_____s watching their

micro_____. Soon the space_____ would roar upwards

at super_____ speed. It seemed difficult to imagine that it was nearly

forty years since the launching of *Sputnik I*, the first satellite to orbit the earth.

Name

Objective: Learn meanings of words by looking at their etymology.

Unit 35

Where does it come from?

 Many modern English words are made from Latin or Greek words. For example: the word **astronaut** comes from two Greek words, **astron** meaning 'a star' and **nautes** meaning 'a sailor'. So we could say that an astronaut is a 'space sailor'!

1. Work out the meanings of the words in bold. The first one has been done for you.

If **astro** means 'star' and **naut** means 'sailor',   **astronaut** means

space sailor

If **cosmo** means 'universe' and **naut** means 'sailor',   **cosmonaut** means

_____

If **lumin** means 'light' and **ous** means 'full of',   **luminous** means

_____

If **trans** means 'across' and **mit** means 'send',   **to transmit** means

_____

2. Check your answers in a dictionary. Add any new words, with their meanings, to your wordbank.

 Many English words come from foreign words. Sometimes the original word from the foreign language is spelled a little differently. The English word is said to be **derived** from that word. It is often written like this in a dictionary.

\<L   means 'derived from Latin'

\<Gk means 'derived from Greek'

\<Gk *astron*, a star means 'derived from the Greek word **astron**, a star'

3. Explain what these derivations mean. The first one has been done for you.

\<L *terra*, earth   *from the Latin word "terra", meaning "earth"*

\<L *avis*, bird   _____

\<L *extra*, outside   _____

\<Gk *tekhne*, art   _____

\<Gk *mikros*, small   _____

Name

Objective: Learn meanings of words by looking at their etymology.

ued from P106

Unit 35

4. Make some words from these Latin and Greek roots. One has been done for you. Use a dictionary to check your words.

terra (earth) _territory   territorial   terrestrial_____

avis (bird) _____

bios (life) _____

mikros (tiny) _____

finis (end) _____

ge (earth) _____

5. Fill in the spaces, using the modern English words that have been derived from the Greek or Latin words in the brackets.

Into space

A giant (<Gk *tele*, far: *skopos*, watcher)

_____ allows us to see far

into space. Satellites which (<L *circum*, around;

navigare, to sail) _____ the Earth (<L e, from

or out; *mittere*, send) _____ signals which allow us to

improve (<L *communis*, share) _____. (<Gk

astron, star; *nautikos*, sailor) _____ are also

able to hear what people are telling them on Earth.

6. Read these words aloud, then check their meanings in a dictionary. Add the words to your wordbank, with their meanings.

astronomy	cosmic	aviary	altitude	telescope	biology
aviation	visible	navigate	meteor	microscope	

7. Now write five sentences of your own in your workbook, using some of the new words.

Edit and proof-read

You should always proof-read your writing for mistakes in spelling, punctuation and grammar. A piece of writing may go through many versions or drafts before it is finished. If you know how to mark the changes you wish to make, you will be able to produce the next, improved draft more quickly and easily.

1. Read through the passage, looking carefully at the changes that have been marked. Try to work out what the marks mean.

Why does an astronat see more than one sunrise and sunset in 24 hours?

cap   Here on earth we see one sunset and one sunrise every day – that is, every   (SP)

(SP)   24 hours 26 ours because thats how long it takes the Earth to make one complete turn

l.c.   on its axis. We see a Sunset when the Earth turns away from the sun   (SP) cap

cap   before our side grows dark we see a sunrise when the Earth turns

(SP)   towards the sun just before our side grows bright. A person circling the   (SP)

Earth in a spacecraft does so many times in a 24 hour period. That's 16

times in 24 hours. In fact, it takes only 1.5 hours for a spacecraft to circle.

So an astronaut would see 16 sunrises and 16 sunsets in 24 hours.

Look at the following proof correction marks:
  ⋏   means something is missing.
  ⊙   means a full stop is missing
Where there is a full stop missing, there is also a capital letter missing on the next word. The capital letter is shown like this in the text ≡ and like this *cap* in the margin.
  ,   means an apostrophe is missing.
  (SP) means there is a spelling mistake. You need to find out how to spell that word. When you do, you can write the word correctly above the misspelled word.
  l.c. means the letter should be in lower case.
  ⌒   means that a sentence is in the wrong place. The arrow head shows where it should go.

2. Write the next draft of the passage in your workbook, making all the changes that have been marked. Now read your draft again. Are there any changes you would like to make? If so, make them in a third draft.

Photocopiable Continued on

Objective: Improve writing by replacing overused words with suitable alternatives.

nued from P108

When you proof-read your writing for mistakes in spelling, punctuation and grammar, you should also ask yourself whether the style of your writing could be improved. When we write, we often find ourselves using the same words over and over again. Using different words makes our writing more interesting to read. Overused words can often be replaced by more interesting and specific words which more clearly express exactly what we want to say.

Words or phrases we commonly overuse are **got**, **get**, **getting**, **nice**, **good**, **a lot of**, **say**, **said** and **then**.

3. In these sentences replace the overused words in brackets with a different word (or words) that makes sense. Ask yourself in each case how you can make your meaning clearer and the writing more interesting. But remember that the sentences must make sense!

We (got) a cage for our hamster. _____

On Wednesday, we went to the fairground. We had a (nice) time.

_____

He is reading a (good) book. _____

This cake tastes (good). _____

At the cinema, we bought our tickets. Then we found our seats, (then) we

ate some popcorn, (then) the film began. _____

For my birthday, I (got) (a lot of) presents. _____

We were (getting on) the bus when he saw us. He (said), "Wait for me!"

_____

4. Use your thesaurus or dictionary to find a different word or words for the overused words in these sentences. Write the new sentences in your workbook.

Sam (ate) his ice-cream.   The explorers (went) up the mountain.
Gopal (walked) down the lane.   Alice was angry so she (shut) the door.

Name

rehearse	brick	purpose
panic	ladies	

Look at these words.

Say them aloud.

Cover each set of words.

Write them in your workbook.

Check to see if you are right.

disaster	column	autumn
theatre	neighbour	
dessert	murmur	immerse
fertile	turquoise	
scissors	drive/driving	journey/journeys
key/keys	computer/computing	
metre	grammar	scholar
vicar	radiator	
ceiling	seize	aviary
visible	territory	

When you have written each set of words, CHECK them to see if they are right. If they are right, put a tick. If any are wrong, cross them out. Look carefully at the correct word(s) again, note where you went wrong and write them again in your wordbank.

There are 34 words. How many did you get right first time? Do the same with these sentences. (Don't forget to look at the punctuation!) You can WRITE, then CHECK after each sentence.

 Continued on

1. A space traveller may be called an astronaut or a cosmonaut.

2. People noticed that the scientist had forgotten to remove his white coat.

3. She had a huge telescope in her attic to help her to observe the galaxy.

4. Pilots in aircraft usually give passengers information about the plane's altitude.

5. There have been fantastic achievements in space travel; space travellers have communicated with Earth.

6. The magician possessed a beautiful ring of turquoise; he said it had magical powers.

7. We were so immersed in watching television that we did not hear the faint knocking noise.

8. The boat had capsized and the instructor shouted, "Can you see any survivors in the water?"

9. Our neighbours invited us to their bonfire in late autumn; **bon** is a French word meaning 'good'.

10. The jeweller advised my mother to insure her diamond rings as early as possible.

Look at these sentences.

Say them aloud.

Cover each sentence.

Write them in your workbook.

Check to see if you are right.

Do the same with these sentences. (Don't forget to look at the punctuation!) You can WRITE, then CHECK after each sentence.

How many sentences were correct?

Enter any words that were not correct into your wordbank under the correct letter. Do this even if the word is there already.

Name

Aa
abbreviation
abscess
abundant
accessible
accommodation
accompanied
accompaniment
accompany
accompanying
accomplish
accomplishment
account
accountable
ache
achieve
achievement
acid
acquire
acquit
action
add
added
address
admirable
admire
admission
admit
adolescence
adolescent
advice

advise
advised
adviser
afford
afforded
agile
airport
allow
allowable
allowance
allowed
allowing
almighty
almost
already
altitude
altogether
amaze
amazed
amazing
amuse
amused
ancestor
announce
announced
anything
applicable
application
apply
Arctic
arrange

arrangement
astronomy
athlete
audible
autumn
autumnal
aviary
aviation

Bb
BA
backpack
bad
bake
baked
bald
ballpoint
band
bare
bask
bat
batting
BBC
beautiful
beautifully
bed
bedding
beg
begged
benefit
benefited

benefiting
best
bet
better
betting
bicycle
biology
bird
biscuit
blame
blamed
blight
blossom
blossomed
blossoming
blue
board
bomb
books
bore
bored
bow
bowel
boy
breakfast
brew
bright
brightly
brown
BST
build

building
bump
burglar
burn

Cc
calculate
calculation
cancel
cancelled
cancelling
canoe
capture
captured
careful
carefully
catch
catching
caught
cease
ceased
ceiling
celebrate
celebration
change
changeable
charge
charged
chase
chasing
check-in

Photocopiable ■ SCHOLASTIC Continued on

wordbank

chemicals	comparable	construct	dangerous	doctor
chew	compare	construction	daughter	doe
chocolate	compel	cont.	delicious	dolphin
choice	compete	contraband	delighted	doubt
chop	competition	contradict	depend	doubtful
chopped	complete	contradiction	dependable	drew
circle	completing	contrast	depress	drink
civil	compress	control	depression	drinkable
civility	compression	controlling	deride	drive
climb	compulsion	cook	derision	driven
climbed	computation	cookbook	descend	driving
climbing	compute	cosmic	deserve	drop
clip	computer	count	dessert	dropped
clipping	computing	counted	destroy	drove
clothes	concentrate	courtesy	destroyed	drown
cloud	concentration	cow	destroyer	dumb
clue	concern	credible	destroying	dusk
coffee	conclude	crowd	develop	
coil	conclusion	crowded	development	**Ee**
colourful	concrete	crumb	diamond	Earth
colourfully	condemn	crutches	digest	edible
colt	condemnation	cup	digestible	e.g.
column	condensation	cupboard	digestion	eight
comb	condition	curl	disaster	electrician
combat	confess	curled	discuss	elephant
combination	confession	curve	discussion	embitter
combine	congregate		displace	employed
commission	congregation	**Dd**	displacement	encage
commit	connect	damage	ditch	encamp
communicate	connection	damaging	division	encash
communication	connects	damnation	do	encircle

Continued from P113

encouraged	explain	float	gnaw	headache
endanger	explorer	flounder	gnome	healthier
endangered	expulsion	flower	gnu	healthiest
engine	extend	flowered	good	healthy
engulf	extension	flowering	govern	heard
enjoy		fly	government	height
enjoyment	**Ff**	foil	graceful	heir
entangle	famous	foreign	gracefully	herb
entrance	fast	forget	grammar	higher
environment	faster	forgetting	grew	highest
equate	fastest	fountain	ground	highwayman
equation	fax	fragrant	group	honest
equator	faxed	fried	guilt	honorary
equestrian	faxing	frightened	guilty	honour
equinox	February	fruit	gullies	hop
equip	fertile	fry	gymnasium	hopeful
equipment	fetch	fur	gymnast	hopefully
erode	fibre	further	gymnastics	hopped
erosion	fight			horrible
event	fish			hound
eventful	fit	**Gg**	**Hh**	hurdle
excavate	fitted	gardener	hand	hurl
excavation	fitter	ghastly	handbag	hutch
excellent	fittest	gherkin	handed	hymn
excitable	fixable	ghetto	happier	hymnal
excite	fixes	ghostly	happiest	
excursion	flap	giggle	happy	
expand	flapping	giggling	hatch	**Ii**
expandable	flew	gild	hatching	illustrate
expansion	flexible	gnarled	hate	illustration
expel	flight	gnash	hating	immerse
		gnat	head	immersed

Photocopiable ➤ SCHOLASTIC Continued on

Name

wordbank

immersion
immobile
immune
impatient
important
impossible
impractical
impress
impression
impure
inaccurate
inadequate
include
included
including
inconsistent
incredible
indirect
inert
inflame
inflammable
information
inspector
install
instalment
insufficient
invincible

Jj

January
ewel

joint
joist
journey
journeyed
journeying
journeys
judge
jump
jumped
jumping

Kk

kerb
kernel
key
keys
khaki
kick
kicked
kicking
kidnapped
kidnapper
kidnapping
kitchen
knapsack
knave
knead
knee
knell
knife
knight

knit
knives
knock
knocking
knot
know
knuckle

Ll

laid
lamb
lamp
laptop
latch
lay
laying
learn
lend
lending
lesson
library
limb
lose
losing
low
loyal
lump
lunch

Mm

magician
magnificent
malnutrition
malpractice
manor
marina
marine
mariner
maritime
married
marry
mat
match
mathematician
matted
measure
measurement
melt
merged
meteor
metre
microscope
mighty
mild
milk
mix
mixed
mixing
mobile
model

modelling
moist
monolith
monotone
moonlight
more
most
mow
mowed
mowing
MP
multicoloured
multi-purpose
multiracial
multitude
murder
murky
murmur

Nn

navigate
nearly
neighbour
nightingale
nod
nodded
noise
notable
note
notice
noticing

Continued from P115

wordbank

numb
nurse

Oo

occur
occurred
occurring
ointment
omission
omit
opened
opening
optician
orbit
orbited
orbiting
orphan
out
ozone

Pp

paid
pain
paint
painting
particularly
pass
passable
passing
passport
patch

patient
pay
paying
peacefully
pedal
pedalled
pedalling
permanent
permission
permit
pheasant
phobia
photograph
photography
physical
picture
pin
pinned
plan
planned
plaster
plastered
plastering
player
playful
playfully
pleasant
plight
plug
plugging
plumber

PM
pneumatic
pneumonia
point
pole
postpone
postponement
powder
powdered
powdering
practice
practise
pre-arranged
precaution
precious
precise
precision
precocious
pre-empt
prefer
preferring
prejudge
premature
prepare
prerequisite
prevent
preview
principal
principle
probably
prop

propel
propeller
propelling
propping
propulsion
pseudonym
psychology
pterodactyl
PTO
purchase
purpose
pursue

Qq

quadruple
quadruplicate
quagmire
quail
quaint
quake
qualify
quality
quarantine
quarrel
quarrelled
quarrelling
quarter
query
question
queue
quibble

quickly
quiet
quite
quiver
quiz
quotation
quote

Rr

radiator
ran
raspberry
Rd
read
reason
reasonable
recognise
reed
refer
referred
refrigerator
rehearse
reign
relief
repel
replied
reply
repulsion
reputable
repute
requiem

Photocopiable ▪ SCHOLASTIC Continued o

wordbank

requisition	scholar	shipping	spoilt	study
responsible	science	shirt	spot	studying
ridden	scientific	shoe	spotted	subaqua
ride	scientist	shoulder	spotter	sub-editor
riding	scissors	shout	spotting	submarine
right	scold	shrew	spruce	submerge
risk	scratches	shrewd	spy	submission
rob	screw	sieve	spying	submit
robbed	screwed	sigh	squirm	subordinate
robbing	screwing	sighing	stamp	subterranean
rot	sculptor	sign	steady	subtle
rotted	search	situate	steadying	suburb
round	searching	situation	step	subway
royal	seasick	ski	stepping	subzero
rule	secretary	skilful	stir	sue
rump	seize	skilfully	stirred	suffer
run	semicolon	skirmish	stitch	suffered
running	semi-detached	slam	stop	suffering
	semi-final	slammed	stopping	suitcase
Ss	semiquaver	slew	straight	sun
said	sensible	slide	strait	sunburn
sandwich	sequence	slight	stray	superb
satchel	sequin	soil	strayed	supply
satisfaction	servant	sold	straying	supplying
satisfy	shake	solemn	strength	surplus
Saturday	shape	solemnity	strip	surprise
saucer	shaping	solicitor	stripped	surprising
say	shell	soup	strong	survivor
saying	shellfish	south	stronger	suspicious
scald	ship	sovereign	strongest	swam
scent	shipped	spoil	studies	sweet

Continued from P117

wordbank

sweetly	throwing	tripping	**Ww**	window
swerve	thrown	triumph	wag	wipe
swerved	thumb	tropical	wagged	wiping
swift	Thursday	true	warm	wish
swifter	tightened	try	wash	wishful
swiftest	time	tug	washed	wonder
swim	tip	tugging	washing	wonderful
swimming	tipped	tunnel	watch	work
swum	tired	tunnelling	weigh	workable
	to	turquoise	weight	world
	toaster		weld	worm
Tt	toe		well	worried
tap	toil	**Uu**	welter	worry
tapped	tomb	umbrella	whale	worrying
technician	toothbrush	unique	wheat	worse
telephone	toothpaste	unison	wheels	worship
telescope	top		when	worshippers
temperature	topped		whet	worshipping
temporary	tour	**Vv**	whimper	worst
terrible	tourists	vein	whip	worth
territory	towel	verb	whippet	wrap
theatre	toxic	vessel	whirl	wrapping
there	transfer	vicar	whisk	write
thermal	transferred	victor	whiskers	
thesaurus	travel	vinegar	whisper	
think	travelled	violet	whist	**Yy**
thirst	traveller	VIP	whistle	yield
thirsty	travelling	visible	whistled	
thoroughly	tried	visit	white	
thoroughness	trip	visited	whole	
threw	tripped	visiting	wild	
throw		voice		

Photocopiable   ■ SCHOLASTIC

Objective: Spell words with *o* sounds as in *go, hole, toe, cold, boat, blow, soul.*

Supplementary unit **1** See Unit 1 **page 28**

Sounds like 'go'

1. Find the **o** words in this wordsearch. They all have an **o** sound like **go**. The words go across or down. Shade the boxes or draw a line to show each word you find, and write the words below.

c	l	o	a	k	s	o	o	l	d
c	o	m	b	c	o	v	e	r	d
o	a	e	f	g	a	h	l	j	d
c	n	l	m	n	p	o	a	c	h
o	w	e	o	s	p	q	r	g	o
a	l	t	h	o	u	g	h	s	l
b	l	o	w	u	h	o	l	d	l
o	t	a	u	l	o	a	f	n	o
w	v	d	w	f	o	l	l	o	w
n	x	y	g	h	o	s	t	z	a

*cons = consonant

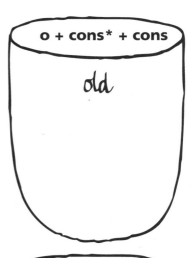

o + cons* + cons

old

oa

cloak

ow

hollow

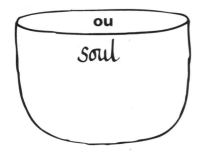

ou

soul

o

so

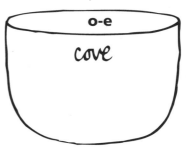

o-e

cove

Photocopiable ♦ SCHOLASTIC

Name

Run, run, run

Remember the 'rule': when we add a suffix to words which end in consonant–vowel–consonant (CVC), we double the final consonant. For example: **run** + ing = ru**nn**ing
          s**pot** + ed = spo**tt**ed

1. Write the correct form of these verbs in the spaces. Be careful! Some of these are not CVC words.

Simon and Javi (decide) _____ to go to the car boot

sale, (travel) _____ by bicycle because it was only a

mile away. Simon made some sandwiches, (cut) _____

the bread very thinly. They (arrive) _____ early and

soon (spot) _____ three of their friends. One of them

had bought a spade for 50p. Then it began to rain and since we had

forgotten our raincoats, we soon became (soak) _____

through. We all rushed home, (cycle) _____ as quickly

as we could!

Name

Objective: Spell different forms of verbs: past tense, present participle and past participle.

Take a walk

1. Read these examples.

present tense	they **walk**
past tense	they **walked**
present participle	they are **walking**
past participle	they had **walked**

2. Fill in the missing parts of these verbs in the grid.

verb	past tense	present participle	past participle
ride			
travel			
cycle			
run			
hike			
swim			
fly			

3. Now write three sentences, using the **present participles** of three of the verbs above.

_____

_____

_____

Name

Faster and faster

Adjectives
describe a person
or thing.
For example:
The train is **slow**.

Adjectives can also compare one thing with another thing. Then the adjective changes.
For example: This train is **slower**, but that train is **slowest**.

We call these adjectives of comparison.

1. Use adjectives of comparison to fill the spaces.

Our car is fast, but the train is f_____, and the plane is

f_____ of all three.

Their brother is healthy, but my brother is h_____, and my

Dad is the h_____ of all of us.

Some adjectives of comparison do not add **er** or **est**.
For example: famous   **more** famous   **most** famous

2. Do the same with these sentences.

I think France is (beautiful) _____ b_____

than Spain.

On motorways, rain can be dangerous, but snow is _____

d_____, and fog is the _____

d_____.

Name

Change it

When we add **ment** to a verb, we change it into a noun.
For example: **to govern** (verb or doing word)
the government (noun or naming word)

1. Read the sentences, then choose verbs from the box and change them into nouns to fill in the spaces.

postpone	measure	arrange	equip
judge	accompany (Take care with this one!)		

There was a _____ of the show due to bad weather.

The _____ of the curtains was 10 metres by 4 metres.

In court, we heard _____ given against the accused.

Please alter our a_____ s; I cannot come on Wednesday.

What kind of _____ do we need for camping?

The pianist was the a_____ to the singer at the concert.

Think of 'oo' words

1. Fill in the crossword to make words with **oo** sounds.

Across

1. The sky is the colour.
2. A type of pine tree. Starts with **spr**.
4. Uncommon.
6. A machine that computes.
7. Delicious for lunch if hot in a bowl. Starts with **s**.
8. People who come to see things in a country (to_____s).
11. You must not break this or you will be in trouble (r_____).
12. A valuable precious stone (j_____el).

Down

1. Very pretty (be_____).
2. Very cunning (shr_____).
3. A number of people together (gr_____p).
5. If everyone sings together they sing in (un_____).
9. Today I throw; yesterday I...
10. Today I grow; yesterday I...

Name

Objective: Add suffixes to words ending in *e, y, w* or *x*.

Fix it

 Remember: when we add a suffix to words that end in **e**, we drop the **e**.
For example: advis**e** advis**ed**   advis**ing**   advis**er**
When we add a suffix to words that end in **w** or **x**, we simply add the suffix.
For example: allo**w**   allow**ed**   allow**ing**   allow**able**   allow**ance**
        fi**x**   fix**es**   fix**ed**   fix**ing**   fix**able**
When we add any suffix except **ing** to words that end in the consonant **y**, we change the **y** to **i**.
For example: stud**y** stud**ied**   stud**ies**   stud**ying**

1. Fill in the spaces in the grid to make new words.

verb	ing	ed
mix		
		surprised
	accompanying	
wipe		
		included
		worried
follow		

2. Use some of the words you have made to complete these sentences.

1. They were _____ their dirty hands.

2. Refreshments are _____ in the price of the ticket.

3. It was quite _____ to find that I had won first prize.

4. Rick's dog _____ him to school yesterday.

5. The singer was _____ by a pianist.

6. We started _____ when Jason did not arrive on time.

7. Oil and water do not _____.

Name

Objective: Change adjectives into adverbs ending in *ly*.

Sing sweetly

Remember: many adverbs end in **ly**.
For example: The man walked slow**ly**.
(The adverb **slowly** tells us about the verb, **walked**.)

When a word ends in **l**, we still add **ly** to make it into an adverb.
For example: The girl was carefu**l**.
(The adjective **careful** tells us about the noun, **girl**.)

The girl listened carefu**lly**.
(The adverb **carefully** tells us about the verb, **listened**.)

1. Complete the grid with the missing adjectives and adverbs.

adjectives	adverbs
bright	
	hopefully
sweet	
	wonderfully
colourful	
peaceful	
skilful	

2. Now complete these sentences, using adjectives or adverbs from the grid.

1. We played (skill) _____ and won the game.

2. Birds sing (sweet) _____.

3. In summer the flowers bloom (colour) _____.

4. Geeta was (hope) _____ of going to stay in Scotland.

5. What a (wonder) _____ surprise!

6. The polished glass shone (bright) _____!

7. Baby Jack sleeps (peace) _____.

Photocopiable **S**CHOLASTIC

Objective: Spell words with the prefixes *em, en, im, in* and *pre*.

Know your prefixes

1. Fill in the crossword with words that have **em**, **en**, **im** and **in** prefixes.

Across

1. Not efficient.
3. Not direct.
4. To view beforehand.
7. Not perishable.
9. Not mobile.
10. Not consistent.
11. If the insect bite doesn't poison you, you are im_____.
12. To form a circle around.

Down

2. Another word meaning to hug (em_____).
5. The opposite of polite.
6. To stop something happening you pre_____ it.
8. Not possible.

Name

Supplementary unit **10** See Unit 11 **page 50**

What a con!

If you know the meanings of prefixes you can spell and understand many more words.
For example: **com** and **con** sometimes mean 'with', so **combine** means 'to join with'.

1. Finish these definitions.

If **com** means 'with' and **battuere**
means 'to beat', the word **combat** means _____.

If **con** means 'with' and **cava** means
'hollow', the word **concave** means _____.

2. Find the meaning of **convex** in a dictionary. Write the word **concave** or **convex** under each drawing.

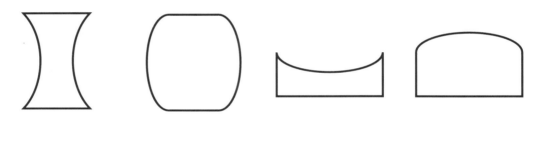

_____ _____ _____ _____

3. Here are some **com** and **con** words. Write the correct one in each space in the sentences below.

compel   condition   concentrate   concrete   connects   concern

You must _____ if you are driving along country roads,

particularly where one _____ with another. City roads are

often made of _____. Country roads are sometimes in bad

_____. It is a real _____ when you are driving.

These roads _____ the driver to be careful.

Photocopiable ■ SCHOLASTIC

Name

Supplementary unit **11** **See Unit 12 page 53**

All at sea

The prefix **sub** comes from a Latin word meaning 'under'. The root **mar** comes from a Latin word meaning 'sea'.

1. Make these **sub** and **mar** words. Write them in the spaces. The first ones have been done for you.

sub		**mar**	
terranean	_Subterranean_	iner	_mariner_
merge	_____	ine	_____
-editor	_____	ina	_____
way	_____	itime	_____

2. Check the meanings of any new words, then complete these sentences. Choose from the words above.

The octopus is a _____ creature.

You should use the _____ to cross that busy road.

The _____ was full of yachts.

A _____ checks news reports for errors.

The old _____ first went to sea when he was 12 years old.

It was exciting to discover a _____ cave at the beach.

The newspaper report said that the ship was completely _____d.

The _____ museum had a painting of Sir Francis Drake.

Photocopiable ■ S C H O L A S T I C

Name

Clouds abound

1. Write the words that rhyme with:

bound

f_____   p_____   gr_____   r_____

h_____   s_____   m_____   w_____

bounce

o_____   p_____   pro_____   tr_____

fl_____   de_____   ann_____

2. Finish these word lists with a word that has an **ow** sound.

East, North, West, S_____

one, ten, hundred, th_____

castle, mansion, h_____, apartment

bedroom, kitchen, l_____

plains, hill, m_____

3. Here is a list of words built on the word **mount**. Choose the correct words to complete the sentences below.

> mountain   mounting   mountainous   mounted

The bikes raced over the most _____ course in the world.

I _____ my pony from the left side.

The car climbed slowly up the _____ road.

The horses were all in the _____ yard.

Photocopiable ◀ SCHOLASTIC

Name

Objectives: Spell words with *silent b*; correct a passage.

Little lambs

1. Complete the crossword. Many of the words have **silent b** in them.

Across

2. An arm is a l_____.
3. It explodes (b_____).
4. A person who fixes the pipes and drains (p_____).
7. If you owe money, you are in d_____.
8. Part of a doorway (j_____).
9. Not able to speak (d_____).
10. A colour.

Down

1. To c_____ a tree.
5. A young sheep (l_____).
6. A bright colour.
8. May, J_____, July.
9. To be unsure; to have d_____.

2. Cross out the incorrect words in this paragraph. Then rewrite it correctly.

We drove sowth down the broun road until we came to a camping grownd. We climed owt of the car and I showted to Dad, "Wear not alloud to camp hear." Dad grould but took know notice. He was a thowsand miles away.

We _____

_____

_____

_____

_____

Name

Objective: Spell words ending in *ible* and *able*.

Supplementary unit 14 See Unit 16 **pages 62–3**

Are you responsible and sensible?

1. Look at these word parts. Decide whether they should have **ible** or **able** added to them. Write down the complete word each time.

respons _____

sens _____

change _____

ed _____

reason _____

dur _____

It is r_____ to expect that I will be home at 4pm.

The weather has been very ch_____.

The toadstools are not e_____.

Who is r_____ for putting out the lights?

She is quite a s_____ girl and has managed to save her pocket money.

If something wears well, and lasts a long time, we say it is d_____.

Scholastic Literacy Skills
Spelling Ages 10–11

Photocopiable ☙ SCHOLASTIC

Name

Sail away

1. Circle the tricky parts of these words. Write sentences, using each of the words, in your workbook.

accommodation	beautiful	descend	entrance	tour
information	gullies	journey	pleasant	sign

LADY DORIS

2. Underline the spelling mistakes in these sentences.

The jerney was plesant and relaxing.

The bus desended into a butiful green vally.

The enterance to the park was blocked by a gullie cawsed by the recent flud.

3. Now write down the sentences, using the correct spellings.

_____

_____

_____

_____

Name

At night

1. Write the correct **ight** word for each of these definitions. They do not all sound the same. The first one has been done for you.

The hours of darkness

_night_____

Very powerful

_____y

How heavy something is

its _____

It has a flashing light to warn ships

l_____

Two times four

_____

An electric flash in the sky

l_____

A disease found in plants

b_____

Of little importance

s_____

Joy

d_____

2. Use your dictionary to check the meanings of any new words.

Name

Fancy that

Many **ph** words come to us from the Greek language and sound like the letter **f**.
For example: **ph**rase

1. Read these **ph** words aloud. Split each word into syllables as you read it. Write the syllables and then the meaning. The first word has been done for you.

word	syllables	meaning
philately	phil at e ly	the collecting of stamps
phoney		
phosphorus		
photograph		
pharmacist		
triumphant		

2. Now fill in the spaces in these sentences, using **ph** words.

They were _____ when they found their way out of the maze.

We asked the _____ what we ought to take for our sore throats.

The boy collected stamps; he had been interested in _____ since he was eight.

P_____ seems to glow in the dark.

He borrowed my camera to take a _____.

These five pound notes are not genuine; they are _____.

Name

Supplementary unit 18   See Unit 22 **page 77**

Past and present

Remember: some verbs change their basic spelling when they are in the past tense. They are called irregular verbs. Regular verbs often just add **ed**.
For example: the verb **to lie** (meaning 'to lie down') is an irregular verb. This is how it changes:

present	past	past participle
I lie	I lay	I (have, had) lain

If the verb **to lie** also means 'to tell a lie', it changes like this:

present	past	past participle
I lie	I lied	I (have, had) lied

If the verb **to lay** (as in 'to lay an egg') is used, it is different again:

present	past	past participle
It lays	It laid	It (has, had) laid

1. Fill in the correct form for each **lie** or **lay** verb in these sentences.

Each night I _____ down to sleep.

Last week I _____ down to sleep.

I have _____ on this bed each time.

You have _____ to me about it.

"I have _____ another egg," clucked the hen. "I _____ each day."

Some other irregular verbs are: **ride   speak   eat**

2. Fill in the gaps in the grid for these irregular verbs.

present	past	past participle
I ride		
	I spoke	
		I (have, had) eaten

Photocopiable ■SCHOLASTIC

Name

Objective: Spell homophones, understanding their meaning.

Supplementary unit **19** See Unit 23 **pages 78–9**

Sounds the same

1. Do this homophone crossword. Check in a dictionary if you are not sure of the meanings of any of the words.

Across
2. A peace/piece of pie.
3. Seas/seize him!
4. Turn right/write/rite here.
7. She rowed/rode/road the boat.
8. The horse's bridal/bridle.
11. The hole/whole cake.
12. A loud grown/groan.
13. A camping site/sight.
14. I am not aloud/allowed to go.

Down
1. He climbed hire/higher and higher/hire.
3. Mandeep found the sauce/source of the river.
5. Go through/threw the park and turn east.
6. The river was wide and the currant/current was strong.
9. They sought legal council/counsel.
10. I like serial/cereal for breakfast.
11. I do not know whether/weather I should go on the trip.

2. Write a story in your workbook, using some of the words from your completed crossword.

Name

Look at the meaning

 Some words have several meanings. We call these words **homonyms**. You need to select the correct meaning for the word you are using.

1. Look up the bold words in a dictionary. Write down the meaning which best fits the word in the sentence.

knit   My mother is going to knit me a sweater.

_____

mail   The knight wore armour made of chain mail.

_____

2. Write a sentence using **mail** another way.

_____

3. Write a sentence using **knit** to mean 'broken bones joining up'.

_____

4. Write three sentences, using the word **punch** to mean:

a hit _____

_____

a drink _____

_____

a thing used to make holes in tickets _____

_____

Photocopiable ☙ SCHOLASTIC

Name

Supplementary unit **21** See Unit 25 **page 84**

Ahoy there!

1. Use lines to join the rhyming words.

boy	point
royal	moist
joint	annoy
joist	loyal
choice	voice

2. Write the rhyming pairs.

_____ _____

_____ _____

_____ _____

_____ _____

_____ _____

3. Find **oy** words in this wordsearch. The words go across or down. Shade the boxes or draw a line to show each word you find, and write the words below.

_____

_____

_____

_____

_____

_____

o	i	n	t	m	e	n	t	k
i	a	c	h	o	i	c	e	o
l	b	b	o	i	l	o	n	i
y	c	v	d	s	o	i	o	u
e	f	o	g	t	i	l	i	t
j	o	y	j	h	n	i	s	u
o	j	a	o	y	s	t	e	r
i	k	g	i	l	o	o	o	e
s	m	e	n	n	i	i	i	o
t	s	p	o	i	l	l	l	p

4. Build word families from these **oy** words. Write them in your workbook. Note any three-syllable words that you have made.

boil	hoist	noise	destroy	join

Name

Tricky words time

1. Look carefully at these tricky words. Examine their difficult parts. Cover them and write them one at a time on the right. Remember to check!

biscuit	(silent **u**)	_____
coffee	(two **f**s, two **e**s)	_____
cupboard	(silent **p**)	_____
fruit	(silent **i**)	_____
knives	(**f** becomes **v**, **silent k**)	_____
refrigerator	(no **d**, and **or** ending)	_____
saucer	(**au** spelling)	_____
scissors	(**silent c**)	_____
sieve	(**i** before **e**)	_____
toaster	(**silent a**)	_____

s	t	o	a	s	t	e	r	s
i	s	a	u	c	e	k	e	i
e	f	r	u	i	t	b	n	s
v	i	o	p	s	q	f	e	c
e	m	o	v	s	u	o	p	u
c	u	p	b	o	a	r	d	i
u	e	a	i	r	i	k	o	t
p	r	n	t	s	t	w	n	m
k	n	i	v	e	s	t	u	l

2. How many tricky words can you find in this wordsearch? The words go across or down. Shade the boxes or draw a line to show each word you find, and write the words below.

_____

_____

_____

_____

_____

Photocopiable ■SCHOLASTIC

Objective: Spell words with *ur* sounds.

It's absurd

Remember: words with an **ur** sound are not always spelled **ur**.
For example: **bird**

1. Complete these words with **ur** sounds.

s_____ve   g_____l   h_____dle   m_____ky

p_____sue   m_____cy   c_____cle   h_____d

2. Now complete this crossword with words
that have **ur** sounds.

Across

3. Not better but w_____e.
5. Absolutely excellent (s_____b).
6. Completely submerged (im_____d).
8. To practise a play (r_____e).
9. To be sure of something (c_____n).

Down

1. A trip (j_____y).
2. Today I hear; yesterday I_____.
4. Extremely polite (co_____s).
7. A sound made by water when it goes
down the plughole (g_____gle).

Name

Objective: Revise useful tips to help with spelling.

Supplementary unit **24** See Unit 33 **pages 102–3**

Remember the 'rules'

● Drop the final **e** when adding a suffix that starts with a vowel.
For example: lov**e** – lov**i**ng *but* lov**e** – lov**ely**

● If the last three letters of a word end in a consonant/vowel/consonant (CVC), the last consonant is doubled when a suffix is added.

Such as: d**rop** – d**ropp**ing tra**vel** – tra**vell**ed *but* dr**eam** – dr**eam**ing
There are exceptions such as orbi**t** – orbi**t**ing, but there are not many of these.

● In many words **i** comes before **e**.
For example: fr**ie**nd gr**ie**f bel**ie**ve
There are exceptions, such as th**ei**r, r**ei**gn, sl**ei**gh, prot**ei**n.
The good news is that after **c** the **e** nearly always comes before **i**.
For example: rec**ei**ve – rec**ei**pt dec**ei**ve – dec**ei**t c**ei**ling – conc**ei**t

● If you hear the sound **k** (or **hard c**) at the end of a word with more than one syllable it is nearly always spelled with a **c**.
For example: pani**c** toni**c** criti**c**
Words of one syllable nearly always end in **ck**.
For example: du**ck** bri**ck** lo**ck** sa**ck**
Words with one syllable and a long vowel sound nearly always end in **k**.
For example: hoo**k** boo**k** too**k** loo**k** bea**k** spea**k**

1. Complete these words correctly. Cover the top of this page!

forget + ing _____   bel_____ve   _____

practise + ing _____   rec_____ve   _____

make + ing _____   gr_____f   _____

seize + ing _____   pani_____   _____

shovel + ed _____   so_____ (**c, ck** or **k?**) _____

carry + ing _____   franti_____   _____

h_____ght _____   broo_____ (**c, ck** or **k?**) _____

2. Check your answers are correct. When they are, write short sentences in your workbook, using the completed words.

Photocopiable ☙ SCHOLASTIC

Name

Supplementary unit 25 See Unit 34 **pages 104–5**

Pair them off

Some new words are not joined together, but they work in pairs. **Moon walk** is an example. Draw lines between the words below to show those that make word phrases like **moon walk**. One has been done for you.

launch	off
moon	satellite
space	walk
mother	thrust
blast	station
cosmic	landing
space	pad
reverse	capsule
command	rays
moon	ship
space	field
multi-stage	rendezvous
communication	shuttle
magnetic	module
space	rocket

2. Complete these sentences, using the correct words.

Now they were flying through space; the _____ pad was far behind. The blast

_____ had been no problem; what would re-entry be like, though? They hoped the

_____ thrust would slow them enough. But first the moon _____

and the moon _____; and the rendezvous with the command _____.

There was so much to achieve. Thank goodness for the communication _____

which kept them in touch with Earth. After this, a trip on the space sh_____ would

be like walking the dog! The early stage of the multi-stage _____ had

left them; the moon was coming closer.

Supplementary unit **26** See Unit 35 **pages 106–7**

A space adventure

1. Read all these words with your teacher. Discuss their meanings.

particles	gravity	retro-rocket	explorer	oxygen
astronaut	galaxy	universe	cosmonaut	Apollo
rendezvous	capsule	thrust	propulsion	telescope
atmosphere	planet	launch pad	countdown	parachute

1. Complete the sentences below. Choose from the words above.

A space traveller is called an astro_____ or a cos_____.

A meeting place in space is often called a ren_____. (The word comes from two French words, **rendez** and **vous**, meaning 'to present yourself'.)

You can see far off pl_____s with a tel_____.

When a space cap_____ comes back to Earth, a

ret_____t is fired to slow the pull of gr_____. Then

a par_____ opens to allow the capsule to land gently after it

enters the Earth's atm_____.

Rocket fuel, when ignited, provides thr_____. It is the form of

propu_____ used at the lau_____ p_____.

2. Using some of the words above, write your own story about a space adventure. Write it in your workbook.

3. When you have finished your story, exchange it with a partner's so that you can check each other's spellings, punctuation and use of capitals. Check, too, for any words left out.